Better Homes and Gardens®

FONDUE

and

TABLETOP COOKING

BETTER HOMES AND GARDENS BOOKS

NEW YORK   DES MOINES

CONTENTS

FOCUS ON FONDUE

The ABC's of Fondue...6
Prize First Courses...8
Cooking Meat, Fish, and Seafood................................14
Dipping into the Cheese Pot....................................26
Fondue Meal Cappers...34

CHAFING DISH TREASURY

A Dish with Many Uses..42
Appetite Tempters...44
Main Dishes—Simple and Gourmet................................50
Desserts to Dazzle..60

TABLETOP CUISINE

Cooking Units Come to the Table................................68
Electric Skillet Time-Savers..................................72
Waffles That Bake Where You Eat...............................82
Griddle Specialties...86

On the cover: Beef Fondue builds enthusiastic chatter as robust appetites await cooked tenderloin cubes. Red Sauce and Garlic Butter complement the savory bites.

To the left: Glossy-sauced pineapple tidbits and apricot halves crown this flaming Chicken Fantasia. The chicken breasts hide slices of ham that are rolled inside.

Our seal assures you that every recipe in *Fondue and Tabletop Cooking* is endorsed by the Better Homes and Gardens Test Kitchen. Each recipe is tested for family appeal, practicality, and deliciousness.

BETTER HOMES AND GARDENS BOOKS

Editorial Director: Don Dooley
Managing Editor: Malcolm E. Robinson   Art Director: John Berg
Food Editor: Nancy Morton
Senior Food Editor: Joyce Trollope
Associate Editors: Nancy Byal, Sharyl Heiken, Rosalie Riglin
Assistant Editors: Sandra Mapes, Elizabeth Strait
Copy Editor: Lawrence Clayton
Designers: Arthur Riser, Harijs Priekulis, Tonya Rodriguez

FOCUS ON FONDUE

Tired of working in the kitchen? Then bring fondue to the table. You needn't wait for a party, or for family guests to arrive. Any time is the right time to cook-at-the-table with fondue.

Fondues give menus seemingly new and exciting twists, yet the idea originated long ago. Out of a fervent desire to utilize hardened cheese and bread, the Swiss concocted a mouth-watering cheese-wine mixture. The cheese was melted in wine, and the bread cubes were then dunked in the mixture. The name *fondue* came from the French word *fondre* which means "to melt."

In this section we have put together the most widely acclaimed fondues from appetizers through desserts. Along with the menu plans, experiment with these recipes and you'll become an effervescent, day-by-day fondue hostess.

The variety of fondue is exemplified by these ingredients for meat, cheese, and dessert fondues. The gleaming fondue pot and long-handled forks are essential equipment for all three types.

THE ABC's OF FONDUE

Learning the hows, whys, and whats of fondue cooking is essential to producing exquisite fondue meals for the first as well as successive times. Check the following pages for facts, hints, and ideas on using your equipment efficiently and safely. With this information at hand, you can confidently dazzle your family and friends with unique fondue dishes.

TYPES OF FONDUE POTS

There are many fondue units now on the market. Each includes a fondue pot, a stand on which the pot rests, and a burner for cooking or keeping the fondue mixture hot. Of the many shapes, sizes, and colors available, fondue units may be grouped into three basic types: metal cookers, ceramic pots, and dessert pots.

If you are seeking an all-purpose piece of equipment, the metal cooker is the most versatile fondue container because so many foods can be cooked in it. The materials most frequently used are stainless steel, plain and colored aluminum, copper, and sterling silver. Since metal can withstand very high heat, this container is best suited for fondues that must be cooked in hot oil—meat fondue, for example —and by turning the heat down, it is also appropriate for cheese or dessert fondue. Allow one fondue cooker for every four persons when serving a hot-oil fondue. The oil will not stay hot enough to cook the food when more than four cook in the same container.

The shape, metal gauge, and added features of the metal container are important selection points to consider. A bowl-shaped cooker that is larger at the bottom than at the top does a good job of containing hot and possibly spattering oil. (Add 1 teaspoon salt to the hot oil to reduce spatters.) A heavy-gauge metal insures even heat distribution. Interior non-stick coatings, available on some cookers, can make cooking and cleaning easier.

The attractively-decorated ceramic, pottery, or earthenware pot most closely duplicates the original Swiss caquelon used for cheese fondue. Shaped like a shallow casserole dish with a handle, the pot's added surface area provides the room needed for swirling a cheese or sauce-type dessert fondue. The ceramic pot, however, should never be used for a hot-oil fondue as the intensive heat will cause the pot to crack. A fondue pot of this style can efficiently serve six to eight at sit-down dinners and more at buffets since no actual tabletop cooking is involved.

Smallest of the containers, the dessert fondue pot is specially designed to hold rich, saucy mixtures. For this reason, the container is considerably smaller in size than either of the previously mentioned pots. A candle warmer adequately keeps the dessert mixture hot whether the container is metal or ceramic. Like the large ceramic container, one dessert pot will serve six to eight people.

Whichever fondue unit you own, be certain to read its use-and-care booklet prior to planning the fondue party, and learn the dos and

On the right: This metal fondue cooker is designed with burner and heat-proof tray. (Remove cover when heating oil.) Beside cooker is a sectioned fondue plate.

In the center: A small dessert pot holds a sauce-type mixture kept warm by means of a candle. Pieces of fruit or cake are dipped in the luscious sauce.

At far right: The ceramic pot is well shaped for swirling foods in cheese or saucy dessert mixtures. Ceramic containers cannot be used for hot-oil fondues.

don'ts of that particular fondue pot. Plan to set the unit on a heat-proof tray (some units include a tray) or mat to protect the table from spattering oil, spills, or heat from the burner. After the meal, allow the pot to come to room temperature before cleaning.

TYPES OF BURNERS

Alcohol, canned heat, and candles are the most common heat sources used in fondue units. However, the popularity of a thermostatically-controlled electric burner is ever increasing. Candle warmers are applicable only to sauce-type dessert fondues as the heat is not sufficient to cook meat or cheese. Most burners provide some means of regulating the amount of heat released. For specific information on how to use these burners, see pages 42-43.

FONDUE ACCESSORIES

In addition to the fondue unit, fondue forks or sturdy bamboo skewers are the only other necessity. Fondue plates are an added convenience but not indispensable.

The fondue fork consists of a long metal shaft with two or three tines at one end for spearing the food and a handle at the other end. Since metal transfers heat quickly, the handle should be made of an insulating material such as plastic or wood. A color-keyed handle tip found on some fondue forks helps the diner identify and keep one fork throughout the meal.

By providing separate compartments for each food, fondue plates eliminate the inter-mingling of highly diverse sauces. Whether china, pottery, or plastic, these plates, available in a wide color assortment, can add a stunning touch to the table setting.

SAFETY TIPS

Safety techniques similar to those developed in kitchen cooking should be maintained when cooking at the table. Although the possibility of flare-ups or burns is remote, the old adage "an ounce of prevention is worth a pound of cure" still prevails in this cooking situation.

The important aspect in tabletop cooking is that you be in complete control of the cooking. A sturdy fondue stand and level table reduce the chances of accidental tipping. Set the fondue unit out of the reach of young children to avoid their quick, unpredictable movements. In fact, fondue is most easily served at an all-adult party. Then serve the children a pre-cooked fondue or other menu ahead of time.

Safety equipment should be available at all times. Should a flare-up develop during dinner, smother the flames quickly by sliding the cover of the fondue or chafing dish over the burning area or by tossing handfuls of baking soda at the base of the flames. In addition, a fire extinguisher should be as easily accessible to the dining area as it is to other parts of the house.

Occasionally a finger may be burned from contact with the hot equipment or hot food. Minor burns can be treated by running cold water over the burn for 15 to 20 minutes, then drying and dressing it with dry gauze. Needless to say, more extensive burns should receive a doctor's prompt medical attention.

PRIZE FIRST COURSES

REUBEN APPETIZERS

- 1 3-ounce package cream cheese, softened
- 1 teaspoon instant minced onion
- 1 16-ounce can sauerkraut, well-drained and chopped
- 1 12-ounce can corned beef
- ¼ cup fine dry bread crumbs

• • •

- ½ cup all-purpose flour
- ½ cup evaporated milk
- ¾ cup fine dry bread crumbs
  Salad oil

Combine cream cheese and onion. Add sauerkraut, corned beef, and the ¼ cup bread crumbs; mix well. Shape into 1-inch balls. Roll in flour; dip in milk, then in the remaining ¾ cup bread crumbs.

Pour salad oil into fondue cooker to no more than ½ capacity or to depth of 2 inches. Heat over range to 375°. Add 1 teaspoon salt. Transfer cooker to fondue burner. Have appetizers at room temperature in serving bowl. Spear with fondue fork; fry in hot oil for 1 to 2 minutes. Transfer to dinner fork before eating. Makes about 100 appetizers.

CRAB-POTATO NIBBLERS

Prepare 2 servings of packaged instant mashed potatoes according to package directions, using *2 tablespoons less milk* than called for, and adding 1 teaspoon instant minced onion to water before boiling. Stir in 1¼ teaspoons Worcestershire sauce, ⅛ teaspoon garlic powder, and dash white pepper.

Add one 7½-ounce can crab meat, drained, flaked, and cartilage removed. Shape into bite-size balls; dip into 1 slightly beaten egg, then roll in ½ cup fine dry bread crumbs.

Pour salad oil into fondue cooker to no more than ½ capacity or to depth of 2 inches. Heat over range to 375°. Add 1 teaspoon salt. Transfer cooker to fondue burner. Have appetizers at room temperature. Spear with fondue fork; fry in hot oil for 2 to 3 minutes. Transfer to dinner fork before eating. Makes 36 appetizers.

COCKTAIL MEATBALLS

Combine 1 beaten egg; 2 tablespoons fine dry bread crumbs; 1 tablespoon finely chopped onion; 2 teaspoons capers, drained; ½ teaspoon salt; ¼ teaspoon dried thyme leaves, crushed; and dash pepper. Add ½ pound ground beef; mix well. Form into ¾-inch meatballs.

Pour salad oil into fondue cooker to no more than ½ capacity or to depth of 2 inches. Heat over range to 350°. Add 1 teaspoon salt. Transfer cooker to fondue burner. Have meatballs at room temperature in serving bowl. Spear meatball with fondue fork; fry in hot oil about 1 minute. Transfer to dinner fork; dip in sauce. Makes about 60 meatballs.

Suggested sauces: Creamy Catsup Sauce, Spicy Tomato Sauce, Mustard Sauce.

FRUITED HAM BALLS

- ½ pound ground fully-cooked ham (about 1½ cups)
- ½ cup soft bread crumbs
- ¼ cup dairy sour cream
- 2 teaspoons finely chopped onion
- ½ teaspoon prepared horseradish
- 1 8¾-ounce can pineapple tidbits, well-drained and halved

• • •

- 1 beaten egg
- ½ cup fine dry bread crumbs
  Salad oil

Combine ham, soft bread crumbs, sour cream, onion, and horseradish; chill. Shape about 1 teaspoon ham mixture around each pineapple tidbit half. Dip in egg, then in dry bread crumbs. Let stand a few minutes.

Pour salad oil into fondue cooker to no more than ½ capacity or to depth of 2 inches. Heat over range to 375°. Add 1 teaspoon salt. Transfer cooker to fondue burner. Have ham balls at room temperature in serving bowl. Spear with fondue fork; fry in hot oil about 2 minutes. Transfer to dinner fork; dip in sauce. Makes about 48 meatballs.

Suggested sauces: Horseradish Sauce, Mustard Sauce, Spicy Pineapple Sauce.

TINY PRONTO PUPS

    1 cup milk
    2 beaten eggs
    2 tablespoons salad oil
    ½ teaspoon prepared mustard
    1½ cups pancake mix
        . . .
    1 5½-ounce package cocktail frank-
        furters (16), halved crosswise*
        Salad oil

Combine first 4 ingredients; add pancake mix. Beat with rotary beater till smooth.

Pour salad oil into fondue cooker to no more than ½ capacity or to depth of 2 inches. Heat over range to 375°. Add 1 teaspoon salt. Transfer cooker to fondue burner. Have meat at room temperature in serving bowl. Spear a frank with fondue fork, dip into batter, letting excess drip off. (If batter thickens, add a little milk.) Fry in hot oil about 1 minute. Transfer to dinner fork; dip in sauce.

*Or substitute regular frankfurters, cut in 1-inch pieces.

Suggested sauces: Mustard Sauce, Horse-radish Sauce, warmed extra-hot catsup.

CRUSTY VEGETABLE BITES

    1 cup fine dry bread crumbs
    ¼ cup grated Parmesan cheese
    1 teaspoon paprika
    1 teaspoon salt
    2 slightly beaten eggs
    1 cup bite-size raw cauliflowerets
    1 cup crosswise-sliced carrots
    1 cup peeled eggplant cut in
        1-inch cubes
        Salad oil

Combine bread crumbs, cheese, paprika, and ½ *teaspoon* salt. Combine eggs, 1 tablespoon water, and remaining salt. Dip vegetables in egg, then in crumb mixture; repeat dipping.

Pour salad oil into fondue cooker to no more than ½ capacity or to depth of 2 inches. Heat over range to 375°. Transfer cooker to fondue burner. Have vegetables at room temperature in serving bowl. Spear vegetables with fondue fork; fry in hot oil for 2 to 3 minutes. Transfer hot, browned vegetable bites to dinner fork before eating. Makes 6 to 8 servings.

SHRIMP TOAST

Finely chop or grind 1 pound cleaned, peeled, uncooked shrimp. Add 3 tablespoons finely chopped onion, 1 beaten egg, 1 teaspoon all-purpose flour, 2 teaspoons lemon juice, ¾ teaspoon salt, and dash pepper. Trim crusts from 6 slices bread; cut each slice into 4 pieces. Spread shrimp mixture on *both sides* of bread.

Pour salad oil into fondue cooker to no more than ½ capacity or to depth of 2 inches. Heat over range to 375°. Add 1 teaspoon salt. Transfer to fondue burner. Have shrimp bread at room temperature. Spear with fondue fork; fry in hot oil for 1 to 2 minutes. Transfer to dinner fork before eating. Makes 24 appetizers.

BACON-WRAPPED CHICKEN

Cut 3 medium chicken breasts, skinned, boned, and cooked, into ¾-inch cubes. Combine ¼ cup soy sauce, 2 tablespoons dry sherry, 1 tablespoon sugar, 1 tablespoon vinegar, and ¼ teaspoon ground ginger; mix well. Add cubed chicken; let stand 30 minutes at room temperature, turning occasionally. Drain well.

Cut *each* of 6 slices bacon in thirds crosswise then in half lengthwise (36 pieces). Wrap one piece around each chicken cube, securing with end of bamboo skewer. Chill thoroughly, at least 1 hour before cooking.

Pour salad oil into fondue cooker to no more than ½ capacity or to depth of 2 inches. Heat over range to 375°. Add 1 teaspoon salt. Transfer cooker to fondue burner. Have meat at room temperature on serving plate. Fry chicken cubes in hot oil about 1 minute or till the bacon is cooked. Makes 36 appetizers.

INDIAN CURRY DIP

In saucepan melt 1 tablespoon butter. Add 1 teaspoon curry powder, ¼ teaspoon *each* salt and garlic powder; mix well. Blend 3 tablespoons cornstarch with one 13¾-ounce can chicken broth (1¾ cups); add to butter mixture. Cook and stir till thickened and bubbly. Pour into fondue pot; set over fondue burner.

Stir in ¼ cup catsup; add ½ cup dairy sour cream. Heat through. Serve hot as dip with cooked turkey cubes, cooked shrimp, or assorted crackers. Makes 2 cups.

THE BUFFET FONDUE

Start with a finger-food buffet featuring three hot dips served in fondue pots, add an activity —party games—and you have an evening with food and fun that everyone can enjoy.

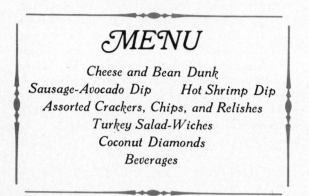

MENU

Cheese and Bean Dunk
Sausage-Avocado Dip   Hot Shrimp Dip
Assorted Crackers, Chips, and Relishes
Turkey Salad-Wiches
Coconut Diamonds
Beverages

This play-and-buffet party can be set up for as many people as you have room to seat. Set up several tables of chance-, concentration-, pencil-and-paper-, and wit-games, and let guests make a choice. With plenty of food available on the buffet table, guests will feel free to serve themselves whenever they desire.

Liven up this informal party with bright colored table decorations. For the buffet centerpiece, glue colored paper cups end-to-end to hold attractively-arranged flowers. Add big stacks of paper plates, cups, and napkins, color-keyed to the centerpiece.

Since this buffet features finger foods, spoons for the sugar and cream users are the only eating utensils needed. Colorful trays to carry food from buffet to game table are nice additions but by no means necessities.

A list of things-to-buy-and-do for the party is essential to even the most experienced hostess. For this party include the following: paper plates, paper cups, paper napkins, three fondue pots, fuel to keep the fondue burners lit several hours, table covers for buffet and game tables, game tables, chairs, party games, centerpiece, assorted crackers and chips, assorted relishes, and the ingredients for the sandwiches, cookies, and three hot fondue dips.

Early on the party day, prepare the sandwich filling and rolls; cut the relishes; bake the cookies; and prepare the dips. Store each food appropriately to maintain high quality. The game tables can be set up any time before the party, scattered in the entertainment area and within easy reach of the buffet table.

Shortly before serving, reheat the dips, pour into fondue pots, and place over fondue burners. Fill the rolls with the sandwich mixture. Then arrange the food along the buffet table to assure a smooth flow: plates; napkins; hot dips with assorted crackers, chips, and relishes; sandwiches; cookies; beverage cups; beverages; sugar, cream, and spoons, if necessary; and trays, if desired. As the party progresses, replenish the buffet table from the kitchen.

HOT SHRIMP DIP

    1 8-ounce package cream cheese
    1 10½-ounce can condensed
        cream of shrimp soup
    ½ cup dairy sour cream
    1 teaspoon prepared horseradish
    ¼ teaspoon Worcestershire sauce

Heat cream cheese till softened. Blend in cream of shrimp soup, sour cream, horseradish, and Worcestershire sauce. Transfer to fondue pot; place over fondue burner. Garnish with cooked, peeled shrimp, if desired. Makes 2 cups.

CHEESE AND BEAN DUNK

Cut one 6-ounce roll garlic cheese food into chunks. Place in saucepan with one 11½-ounce can condensed bean with bacon soup. Heat slowly, stirring constantly, till blended. Stir in 1 cup dairy sour cream and 2 tablespoons sliced green onion. Heat through. Transfer to fondue pot; place over fondue burner. Garnish with sliced green onion. Makes 2⅔ cups.

SAUSAGE-AVOCADO DIP

Cook ½ pound bulk pork sausage, breaking it up into fine particles. Drain off fat; drain cooked sausage well on paper toweling.

In saucepan combine 1 cup mashed avocado, ½ cup dairy sour cream, ⅓ cup orange juice, 1 teaspoon lemon juice, and ¼ teaspoon salt. Add sausage; heat. Transfer to fondue pot; place over fondue burner. Garnish with a lemon twist. Makes about 2 cups.

TURKEY SALADWICHES

    5 cups diced cooked turkey
1½ cups finely chopped celery
  ½ cup toasted chopped almonds
  ¼ cup *each* chopped onion, chopped
      green pepper, and chopped
      canned pimiento
  ¼ cup lemon juice
1⅓ cups mayonnaise
 16 hard rolls, halved lengthwise

In large bowl combine first 7 ingredients and ½ teaspoon salt. Blend in mayonnaise; chill. Scoop out center of roll halves to make slight hollow; toast. Fill each half with about ½ cup turkey mixture. Makes 16 servings.

COCONUT DIAMONDS

In mixing bowl cream together ¾ cup butter or margarine, softened; ½ cup granulated sugar; and ½ teaspoon salt. Stir in 2 cups sifted all-purpose flour. Divide dough in half. Pat *each half* onto bottom of 9x9x2-inch pan. Bake at 350° for 15 minutes or till lightly browned.

Meanwhile in mixing bowl, beat 4 eggs slightly; add 2 teaspoons vanilla. Gradually add 2 cups brown sugar, beating just till blended. Add ¼ cup sifted all-purpose flour and 1 teaspoon salt. Stir in 2 cups flaked coconut and 1 cup coarsely chopped walnuts.

Spread *half* over each baked layer. Bake 20 minutes longer or till wooden pick comes out clean. Cool. Cut in diamonds. Makes 3 dozen.

Entice your guests with a trio of pert and saucy hot dips. Assorted crackers and crisp relishes serve as handy dippers for Cheese and Bean Dunk flecked with green onion. Tasty Sausage-Avocado Dip sporting a twist of lemon and creamy Hot Shrimp Dip complete the tempting threesome.

A WINE-TASTING PARTY

Merge fondue and wine for a stimulating party idea adaptable to any size group. Tasting and talking keep guests busy from start to finish.

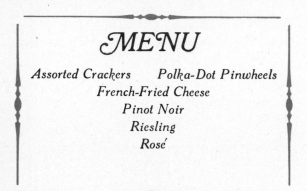

MENU

Assorted Crackers   Polka-Dot Pinwheels
French-Fried Cheese
Pinot Noir
Riesling
Rosé

Wine-tasting parties for the non-connoisseur should be practical and simple so that guests can learn to identify their preferences. Invite only as many guests as can move comfortably about the room, and buy only a few wines.

Select some recognized sweet or dry wines, for example, a Pinot Noir, Riesling, and a Rosé (see Wine Guide, page 32). The average wine-taster can compare different groups of wines, and the connoisseur two or more wines in each category. Either way, allow a total of one fifth (25.6 ounces) for every two people.

A wine-taster's palate perks up with intermittent food refreshers like crackers, cheese, and simple bread appetizers. French-Fried Cheese, fondue-style, reinforces the casual drink-and-eat-when-you-like atmosphere.

Table decorations using empty wine bottles as candle holders with grape-like vines and leaves, carry forth the wine theme. Provide a guideline list for judging, pencils, and simple yet cleverly-designed scorecards for tasters to jot notes on. The remaining buffet-like setting provides essentials; wine, one glass per person, a pitcher of water for rinsing glasses, a container for rinse water, disposable towels for drying glasses, and napkins. Also needed are one fondue cooker for every eight people, fondue forks (bamboo skewers for a large group), and small plates.

Preparing ahead enables the hostess to enjoy the party, too. Make Polka-Dot Pinwheels; coat, then chill cheese for French-Fried Cheese.

The table can be arranged, remembering there will be considerable activity in that area. White and rosé wines should be chilled, red ones opened an hour ahead for full flavor.

At tasting time, bring on the wine, fondue cooker, and food. Via scorecards and chatter, rate wines on appearance, aroma, and flavor. For added challenge, have tasters identify the white, red, and rosé while blindfolded.

FRENCH-FRIED CHEESE

**Assorted *natural* cheeses, cut
in ½ inch cubes***
Beaten egg
Fine dry bread crumbs
Salad oil

For soft cheeses shape crust around soft center as much as possible. Dip in egg, then crumbs; repeat for second layer. (A thick coating prevents the cheese from leaking through.)

Pour oil into fondue cooker to no more than ½ capacity. Heat on range to 375°. Add 1 teaspoon salt. Transfer cooker to fondue burner. Spear cheese with fondue fork; fry in hot oil ½ minute. Cool slightly before eating.

*Use soft cheeses with a crust (Camembert or Brie), semi-hard (Bel Paese or Brick), or hard (Cheddar, Edam, and Gouda) cheeses.

POLKA-DOT PINWHEELS

Have bakery cut 1 unsliced loaf white bread lengthwise in ¼-inch-thick slices. Spread one side of slices with softened butter. Combine two 4¾-ounce cans chicken spread, ¼ cup mashed canned pimiento, and ½ teaspoon curry powder; mix thoroughly.

Spread buttered side of each slice with 3 tablespoons filling. Trim crusts. Place 5 thin green pepper strips, equal distance apart, atop filling of each. Roll up, beginning at narrow end. Wrap in foil or clear plastic wrap; chill. Slice ⅜-inch thick. Makes about 40 pinwheels.

French-Fried Cheese provides a rare treat amid →
wine tasting. Speared and browned in fondue cooker for only a few seconds, cheese has a crisp, golden coating which conceals a soft and creamy center.

COOKING MEAT, FISH, AND SEAFOOD

Dinner is easy on the hostess when the main dish is meat, fish, or seafood fondue. The hostess sets the table, and the guests do the rest themselves. It's instant fun for everyone.

The traditional fondue recipe in this section is Beef Fondue. Although also called Fondue Bourguignonne (Fondue Burgundian), its connection with Burgundy, a region of France, or Burgundy wine is obscure. Beef Fondue consists of beef cubes cooked in hot oil and then dipped in a zesty sauce. Similar fondues substitute other meat, fish, or seafood for beef.

When planning a fondue meal, allow 3/8 pound trimmed, uncooked meat per person and a fondue cooker for every four people. Provide each person with a fondue fork, plate, dinner fork, napkin, and any other appointments needed for the rest of the meal.

Simple accompaniments are all the hostess need prepare. For a minimum menu, serve a tossed salad to nibble on while the meat is cooking, a light dessert, and a beverage. For a heartier meal, add bread or a cooked vegetable.

One to two hours before the meal, cut meat into bite-size pieces and allow to come to room temperature. At serving time, heat the oil-filled pot over the range, add salt to reduce spattering, and transfer to the fondue burner.

At the table, each person spears a meat cube with a fondue fork or bamboo skewer and cooks it to the desired doneness—"rare" (15 seconds) to "well-done" (about 1 minute). If the oil cools during the meal, reheat over the range.

Salad oil is the oil most frequently used for meat fondue. It is easy to use for cooking, and does not flavor the food. Though less popular, peanut oil, a blend of about 3 parts oil to 1 part clarified butter*, and olive oil are sometimes chosen. Like salad oil, peanut oil does not flavor the meat. The butter-oil mixture, however, has a buttery aroma and gives the

meat a slight richness. Olive oil's characteristic flavor carries over to the meat and it smokes more readily than the other oils.

*To clarify butter, melt over low heat; cool. Pour off oily top layer; discard bottom layer.

BEEF FONDUE

> Salad oil
> 1½ pounds trimmed beef tenderloin,
>   cut in ¾-inch cubes

Pour oil into fondue cooker to no more than ½ capacity or to a depth of 2 inches. Heat over range to 425°. Add 1 teaspoon salt. Transfer cooker to fondue burner. Have beef at room temperature. Spear meat with fondue fork; fry in hot oil to desired doneness. Transfer to dinner fork and dip in sauce. Serves 4.

Suggested sauces: Green Goddess Sauce, Olive Sauce, Caper Sauce, Wine Sauce, Mushroom Sauce, Horseradish Sauce, Mustard Sauce, Bordelaise Sauce, Garlic Butter.

FISH AND SEAFOOD FONDUE

> ½ pound *each* fish fillets, shelled
>   lobster, peeled and cleaned
>   shrimp, cut in bite-size pieces*
> Salad oil

Drain uncooked fish and seafood thoroughly; pat dry with paper toweling. Pour oil into fondue cooker to no more than ½ capacity or to depth of 2 inches. Heat over range to 375°. Add 1 teaspoon salt. Transfer cooker to fondue burner. Have fish and seafood at room temperature in serving container.

Spear fish with fondue fork; fry in hot oil till lightly browned. Transfer to dinner fork; dip in sauce. Makes 4 servings.

*Some fish such as crabs, oysters, and scallops are not well-suited for fondue.

Suggested sauces: Dill Sauce, Sauce a la Relish, Tartar Sauce, Sweet-Sour Sauce, Cocktail Sauce, Caper Sauce.

← **Capture the mood** of the sea with a Fish and Seafood Fondue. Speared and cooked fondue-style salmon, shrimp, and lobster make savory morsels dunked in sauces—a la Relish, Dill, or Tartar.

PORK OR HAM FONDUE

> Salad oil
> 2 pounds pork tenderloin, trimmed
>   and cut in 1-inch cubes *or*
> 1½ pounds fully cooked
>   ham, cut in ¾-inch cubes

Pour oil into fondue cooker to no more than ½ capacity or to depth of 2 inches. Heat over range to 425°. Add 1 teaspoon salt. Transfer cooker to fondue burner. Have meat at room temperature. Spear meat with fondue fork; fry in hot oil for 2 to 3 minutes. Transfer to dinner fork; dip in sauce. Makes 4 servings.

Suggested sauces: Marmalade Sauce, Onion Sauce, Basil Butter, Mustard Sauce.

VEAL STRIPS

Pound 1½ pounds veal cutlet to about ⅛-inch thickness. Cut in 3x1-inch strips. Combine about ¼ cup all-purpose flour and ¼ teaspoon salt. Coat veal strips with flour mixture; dip in 2 beaten eggs, then in ½ cup fine dry bread crumbs. Loosely thread each strip on bamboo skewer in accordion fashion.

Pour oil into fondue cooker to no more than ½ capacity or to depth of 2 inches. Heat over range to 425°. Add 1 teaspoon salt. Transfer cooker to fondue burner. Have skewered veal at room temperature on serving plate. Fry in hot oil about 1 minute. Dip in sauce. Serves 4.

Suggested sauces: Garlic Butter, Bordelaise Sauce, Anchovy Butter, Spicy Tomato Sauce.

CHICKEN FONDUE

> Salad oil
> 2 pounds chicken breasts, skinned,
>   boned, and cut in ¾-inch cubes

Pour salad oil into fondue cooker to no more than ½ capacity or to depth of 2 inches. Heat over range to 425°. Add 1 teaspoon salt. Transfer cooker to fondue burner. Have chicken cubes at room temperature in serving bowl. Spear cube with fondue fork; fry in hot oil for 2 to 3 minutes. Transfer to dinner fork; dip in sauce. Makes 4 servings.

Suggested sauces: Bearnaise Sauce, Tangy Cranberry Sauce, 1-2-3 Sauce, Curry Sauce.

SAUSAGE MEATBALLS

Brown ½ pound pork sausage, finely crumbled, with ¼ cup finely chopped onion; drain. Add one 14-ounce can sauerkraut, well-drained and snipped, and 2 tablespoons fine bread crumbs.

Combine one 3-ounce package softened cream cheese, 2 tablespoons snipped parsley, 1 teaspoon prepared mustard, ¼ teaspoon garlic salt, and ⅛ teaspoon pepper. Stir into sauerkraut mixture; chill. Shape meat into ¾-inch balls; coat with ¼ cup all-purpose flour. Combine 2 well-beaten eggs and ¼ cup milk. Roll balls in egg, then ¾ cup fine dry bread crumbs.

Pour salad oil into fondue cooker to no more than ½ capacity or to depth of 2 inches. Heat over range to 375°. Add 1 teaspoon salt. Transfer cooker to fondue burner. Have meatballs at room temperature. Spear meatball with fondue fork; fry in hot oil ½ to 1 minute, or till golden. Transfer meatball to dinner fork; dip in desired sauce. Makes 60 meatballs.

Suggested sauces: Sweet-Sour Sauce, Mustard Sauce, Curry Sauce, Creamy Catsup Sauce.

FONDUED FLANK STEAK

The marinade acts as a built-in sauce—

Bias-cut 1 pound flank steak in very thin 3x1-inch strips. Combine ½ cup salad oil; ½ cup dry red wine; 2 tablespoons catsup; 2 tablespoons molasses; 2 tablespoons finely snipped candied ginger; 1 clove garlic, minced; ½ teaspoon salt; ½ teaspoon curry powder; and ½ teaspoon pepper. Pour marinade over flank steak. Cover; marinate 2 hours at room temperature. Drain well; pat dry with toweling. Thread on bamboo skewers accordion style.

Pour salad oil into fondue cooker to no more than ½ capacity or to depth of 2 inches. Heat over range to 425°. Add 1 teaspoon salt. Transfer cooker to fondue burner. Have skewered meat strips at room temperature on serving plate. Fry in hot oil for 1 to 2 minutes, or till desired doneness. Makes 4 servings.

One bite through the crisp bread crumb coating → unmasks the surprise combination of foods in these festive Sausage Meatballs—spicy pork sausage meat, tart sauerkraut, and tangy cream cheese.

FILLED LAMB BALLS

Curry subtly flavors the meat—

    ½ pound ground lamb
    1 tablespoon fine dry bread crumbs
    1 teaspoon minced green onion tops
    ¼ teaspoon curry powder
    2 to 3 ounces natural Swiss cheese,
        cut in ½-inch cubes
      Salad oil

In small mixing bowl combine lamb, bread crumbs, green onion tops, ¼ teaspoon salt, and curry powder. Shape about 1 teaspoon meat mixture around each Swiss cheese cube to make 1-inch meatballs.

Pour salad oil into fondue cooker to no more than ½ capacity or to depth of 2 inches. Heat over range to 375°. Add 1 teaspoon salt. Transfer cooker to fondue burner. Have lamb balls at room temperature in serving bowl. Spear lamb ball with fondue fork; fry in hot oil about 2 minutes or till browned. Transfer to dinner fork before eating. Makes about 32 meatballs.

JAZZY BEEF BITES

Taste like miniature cheeseburgers—

    1 tablespoon catsup
    1 teaspoon prepared horseradish
    1 teaspoon prepared mustard
    ½ teaspoon instant minced onion
    ½ teaspoon salt
    ½ pound ground beef
    ¼ cup fine soft bread crumbs
      Sharp natural Cheddar cheese,
          cut in ¼-inch cubes
      Salad oil

Combine catsup, horseradish, mustard, onion, salt, and dash pepper; let stand 10 minutes. Combine ground beef and bread crumbs; stir in catsup mixture. Shape meat around cheese into ¾-inch balls. Spear on bamboo skewers.

Pour salad oil into fondue cooker to no more than ½ capacity or to depth of 2 inches. Heat over range to 375°. Add 1 teaspoon salt. Transfer cooker to fondue burner. Have meatballs on bamboo skewers at room temperature on serving plate. Fry meatballs in hot oil about 1½ minutes or till done. Makes about 30 meatballs.

MUSHROOM SAUCES

• In small skillet cook 1 cup sliced fresh mushrooms and ¼ cup finely chopped green onion in ¼ cup butter or margarine till just tender. Blend in 4 teaspoons cornstarch. Add ¾ cup red Burgundy, ¾ cup water, 2 tablespoons snipped parsley, ¾ teaspoon salt, and dash pepper; mix well. Cook and stir till thickened and bubbly. Makes 1½ cups.

• Drain one 3-ounce can chopped mushrooms; chop mushrooms more finely. Dissolve 1 beef bouillon cube in ⅔ cup boiling water. In small saucepan melt 2 tablespoons butter or margarine over low heat. Blend in 2 tablespoons all-purpose flour. Add bouillon all at once; mix well. Cook quickly, stirring constantly, till mixture is thickened and bubbly. Stir in ½ cup dairy sour cream, the finely chopped mushrooms, and 2 teaspoons Worcestershire sauce; heat through. Serve hot. Makes about 1⅓ cups.

• In saucepan combine one 10½-ounce can condensed cream of mushroom soup and ½ cup dairy sour cream; heat. Makes about 2¼ cups.

When heating oil for fondue, use a thermometer to assure that the specified temperature has been reached. Do not allow the oil to smoke. If the oil cools over fondue burner, reheat on the range.

TOMATO SAUCES

- **1-2-3 Sauce:** Combine one 12-ounce bottle extra-hot catsup, 3 tablespoons vinegar, 2 teaspoons celery seed, and 1 clove garlic, halved. Chill; remove garlic. Makes 1¼ cups.
- **Creamy Catsup Sauce:** In small mixer bowl beat one 3-ounce package softened cream cheese till fluffy. Gradually blend in ¼ cup dairy sour cream, 2 tablespoons catsup, ¼ teaspoon salt, ¼ teaspoon Worcestershire sauce, and dash bottled hot pepper sauce; mix well. Stir in 2 tablespoons finely chopped green pepper. Makes about 1 cup.
- **Red Sauce:** Combine 3 tablespoons catsup, 3 tablespoons chili sauce, 1½ tablespoons prepared horseradish, 1 teaspoon lemon juice, and dash bottled hot pepper sauce; mix well. Chill. Makes about ½ cup.
- **Spicy Tomato Sauce:** Combine ½ cup dairy sour cream, 2 tablespoons chili sauce, ½ teaspoon prepared horseradish, ¼ teaspoon salt, and dash pepper. Chill. Makes ⅔ cup.
- **Cocktail Sauce:** Combine ¾ cup chili sauce, 2 to 4 tablespoons lemon juice, 1 to 2 tablespoons prepared horseradish, 2 teaspoons Worcestershire sauce, ½ teaspoon grated onion, dash bottled hot pepper sauce; mix well. Add salt to taste. Chill. Makes 1¼ cups.
- **Mexican Hot Sauce:** In saucepan combine 1 cup chili sauce; ¼ cup chopped onion; 3 tablespoons vinegar; 1 tablespoon salad oil; 1 teaspoon brown sugar; 1 clove garlic, crushed; ¼ teaspoon salt; ¼ teaspoon dry mustard; and ¼ teaspoon bottled hot pepper sauce. Bring to boil; simmer 10 minutes, stirring occasionally. Serve warm or cool. Makes 1¼ cups.

SWEET-SOUR SAUCE

    1 cup sugar
    ½ cup white vinegar
    1 tablespoon chopped green pepper
    1 tablespoon chopped canned
        pimiento
    2 teaspoons cornstarch
    1 teaspoon paprika

In saucepan mix first 4 ingredients, ½ cup water, and ½ teaspoon salt; simmer 5 minutes. Combine cornstarch and 1 tablespoon cold water; add to hot mixture. Cook and stir till bubbly. Cool. Add paprika. Makes 1½ cups.

CURRY SAUCE

    3 tablespoons butter or margarine
    1 teaspoon curry powder
    2 tablespoons all-purpose flour
    1 cup milk

Melt butter. Stir in curry; cook for 1 to 2 minutes. Blend in flour, ½ teaspoon salt, and dash pepper. Add milk all at once. Cook and stir till boiling. Serve hot. Makes 1 cup.

BEARNAISE SAUCE

Combine 3 tablespoons tarragon vinegar; 1 teaspoon finely chopped shallots *or* green onion; 4 whole peppercorns, crushed; and Bouquet Garni*. Simmer till liquid is reduced to half. Strain; add 1 tablespoon cold water.

Beat 4 egg yolks in top of double boiler (not over the water). Slowly add herb liquid. Have ½ cup butter at room temperature. Add a few tablespoons butter to egg yolks; place over *hot*, *not boiling*, water. Cook and stir till butter melts and sauce starts to thicken. Continue stirring in butter till all has been used and sauce is smooth as thick cream. Remove from heat. Salt to taste; add 1 teaspoon minced fresh tarragon *or* ¼ teaspoon dried tarragon leaves, crushed. Makes 1 cup.

*Bouquet Garni: Securely tie a few whole tarragon and chervil leaves in cheesecloth.

BORDELAISE SAUCE

    ½ cup fresh mushrooms, chopped, *or*
        1 2-ounce can chopped
        mushrooms
    2 teaspoons butter or margarine
    4 teaspoons cornstarch
    1 cup beef stock
    ¾ teaspoon dried tarragon leaves,
        crushed
    1 tablespoon lemon juice
    1 tablespoon red wine

Cook fresh mushrooms in butter till tender (if canned, combine with melted butter). Mix cornstarch and cool beef stock; add to mushrooms. Cook and stir till boiling. Add remaining ingredients and dash pepper; simmer 5 to 10 minutes. Makes 1 cup.

CHINESE HOT MUSTARD

¼ cup dry mustard
¼ cup boiling water
1 tablespoon salad oil
½ teaspoon salt

Blend mustard and water. Add salad oil and salt. For more yellow color add a little ground turmeric, if desired. Makes ⅛ cup.

MUSTARD SAUCES

• Melt 2 tablespoons butter or margarine in a small saucepan over low heat. Blend in 2 tablespoons all-purpose flour, ¼ teaspoon salt, and dash white pepper. Add 1 cup milk all at once. Cook quickly, stirring constantly, till mixture thickens and bubbles. Remove from heat. Add 1½ to 2 tablespoons prepared mustard; mix well. Serve hot. Makes about 1 cup.
• Combine 2 beaten egg yolks, 1 tablespoon sugar, 3 tablespoons prepared mustard, 2 tablespoons vinegar, 1 tablespoon water, 1 tablespoon butter, 1 tablespoon prepared horseradish, and ½ teaspoon salt in top of double boiler; mix well. Place over boiling water; cook and stir till thickened, about 2 minutes. Remove from heat. Stir vigorously, if necessary, till sauce is smooth. Cool. Fold in ½ cup whipping cream, whipped; refrigerate. Makes 1 cup.
• In small saucepan blend 3 tablespoons dry onion soup mix and ½ cup milk; let stand 5 to 10 minutes. Add 1 cup dairy sour cream and 2 tablespoons prepared mustard. Heat through, stirring occasionally. Makes 1⅓ cups.
• In a jar mix together ½ cup dry mustard and ½ cup vinegar. Cover and let stand overnight. In saucepan beat 1 egg; stir in ¼ cup sugar, dash salt, and mustard mixture. Cook over low heat, stirring constantly, till mixture thickens slightly and coats a spoon; cool. Blend 1 cup mayonnaise or salad dressing into cooled mustard mixture. Makes about 2 cups.

BASIL BUTTER

Cream ½ cup softened butter till fluffy. Beat in 1 teaspoon lemon juice and ¾ teaspoon dried basil leaves, crushed. Keep basil butter at room temperature for at least 1 hour to mellow before serving. Makes ½ cup.

GARLIC BUTTER

½ cup softened butter
1 small clove garlic, minced

Cream butter till fluffy. Add minced garlic. Let mellow at room temperature at least 1 hour before serving. Makes ½ cup.

ANCHOVY BUTTER

With electric mixer beat 2 cups softened butter, one 2-ounce can anchovy fillets, and 2 tablespoons chopped parsley until well blended. Let mellow at room temperature for at least 1 hour before serving. Makes about 2 cups.

HORSERADISH SAUCES

• Fold 3 tablespoons drained prepared horseradish into ½ cup whipping cream, whipped. Add ½ teaspoon salt. Makes about 1 cup.
• Combine 1 cup dairy sour cream, 3 tablespoons drained prepared horseradish, ¼ teaspoon salt, and dash paprika. Chill.
• Whip one 8-ounce package softened cream cheese and 2 to 3 tablespoons prepared horseradish till fluffy. Blend in 2 tablespoons milk. Chill. Makes 1⅓ cups.
• In saucepan melt 3 tablespoons butter or margarine; blend in 1 teaspoon all-purpose flour. Add ¼ cup vinegar, ¼ cup beef broth, ¼ cup prepared horseradish mustard, and 3 tablespoons brown sugar. Cook slowly, stirring constantly, till thickened. Gradually add a little hot mixture to 1 slightly beaten egg yolk; return to hot mixture. Bring sauce to boiling, stirring constantly. Makes 1 cup.

TANGY CRANBERRY SAUCE

½ cup orange juice
1 tablespoon cornstarch
1 16-ounce can whole cranberry
    sauce
1 tablespoon brown sugar
¼ teaspoon ground cinnamon

In saucepan blend orange juice and cornstarch. Add remaining ingredients. Cook, stirring constantly, till thick and bubbly. Makes 2 cups.

SPICY PINEAPPLE SAUCE

    1 beef bouillon cube
    ¾ cup boiling water
    1 13½-ounce can crushed pineapple,
       undrained
    ¼ cup finely crushed gingersnaps
    2 tablespoons vinegar
    Dash pepper
    Dash ground cloves

In saucepan dissolve bouillon cube in boiling water. Put remaining ingredients in blender container; blend 30 seconds. Add to bouillon. Cook and stir till thick. Makes 2 cups.

MARMALADE SAUCE

In small saucepan combine ½ cup orange marmalade, 1 tablespoon soy sauce, ⅛ teaspoon garlic powder, and dash ground ginger; bring to boiling. Blend together 2 tablespoons cornstarch with ⅓ cup cold water. Stir into hot sauce; cook and stir till thickened and bubbly. Add 2 tablespoons lemon juice. Makes 1 cup.

DILL SAUCE

Combine 1 cup dairy sour cream, 1 tablespoon snipped chives, 1 teaspoon vinegar, ½ teaspoon grated onion, ½ teaspoon dried dillweed, and ¼ teaspoon salt; mix well. Makes 1 cup.

ONION SAUCES

• Melt 2 tablespoons butter with 1 tablespoon sugar over low heat, stirring till sugar turns golden, about 5 minutes. Add ½ cup chopped onion; cook 2 minutes more. Blend in 3 tablespoons all-purpose flour; add 1 cup condensed beef broth. Cook and stir till thickened and bubbly. Add 1 tablespoon vinegar. Reduce heat; simmer, covered, 10 minutes. Makes 1 cup.
• Combine ½ cup dairy sour cream, 1 envelope green onion dip mix, ½ teaspoon Worcestershire sauce, and 2 drops bottled hot pepper sauce. Chill thoroughly. Makes ½ cup.
• Blend together 1½ cups dairy sour cream and 2 tablespoons dry onion soup mix. Stir in ½ cup crumbled blue cheese and ⅓ cup chopped walnuts. Chill. Makes 2 cups.

CAPER SAUCE

In small mixing bowl combine 1 cup mayonnaise or salad dressing and 1 tablespoon undrained capers. Makes 1 cup.

GREEN GODDESS SAUCE

    2 3-ounce packages cream cheese,
       softened
    3 tablespoons milk
    2 tablespoons finely snipped chives
    1 tablespoon snipped parsley
    1 teaspoon finely chopped onion
    2 teaspoons anchovy paste

Blend softened cream cheese and milk. Add snipped chives, snipped parsley, chopped onion, and anchovy paste; mix well. Makes 1 cup.

SAUCE A LA RELISH

    1 8-ounce can tomato sauce
    ¼ cup chili sauce
    2 tablespoons finely chopped onion
    2 tablespoons drained pickle relish
    1 tablespoon vinegar
    1 teaspoon Worcestershire sauce
    ½ teaspoon prepared horseradish
    ⅛ teaspoon pepper

In saucepan combine all ingredients. Cook, uncovered, over low heat about 20 minutes, stirring frequently. Makes 1¼ cups.

TARTAR SAUCE

Combine 1 cup mayonnaise or salad dressing, 3 tablespoons finely chopped dill pickle, 1 tablespoon of snipped parsley, 2 teaspoons of chopped canned pimiento, and 1 teaspoon grated onion; chill. Makes 1¼ cups.

OLIVE SAUCE

Blend together ½ cup dairy sour cream and one 3-ounce package softened cream cheese. Fold in 2 tablespoons chopped pimiento-stuffed green olives, 1 tablespoon finely chopped onion, and 1 teaspoon snipped parsley. Makes 1 cup.

PEANUT SAUCE

In bowl combine ¼ cup chunk-style peanut butter; 2 teaspoons soy sauce; 1½ teaspoons water; ¼ teaspoon sugar; ½ clove garlic, minced; and 1 drop bottled hot pepper sauce. Slowly stir in ¼ cup water. Makes ½ cup.

GINGER SOY

In saucepan combine ½ cup soy sauce and 1½ teaspoons ground ginger. Bring to boiling. Serve hot or cold. Makes ½ cup.

CHILI-CHEESE SAUCE

    1 8-ounce can tomatoes
    8 ounces process American cheese,
        shredded (2 cups)
    ⅓ cup finely chopped canned chilies

Drain tomatoes, reserving juice. Finely cut up tomatoes; add cheese, chilies, and ⅓ cup reserved juice. Heat slowly till cheese melts, 10 to 12 minutes, stirring occasionally. Serve warm. (If mixture thickens, stir in a little tomato juice.) Makes 1⅔ cups.

CREAMY AVOCADO SAUCE

Combine 1 cup mashed avocado, ½ cup dairy sour cream, 2 teaspoons lemon juice, ½ teaspoon grated onion, ¼ teaspoon *each* salt and chili powder; chill. Stir in 3 slices bacon, crisp-cooked and crumbled. Garnish with crisp-cooked bacon curl, if desired. Makes 1⅓ cups.

WINE SAUCE

    ¾ cup sauterne
    ¼ cup catsup
    4 teaspoons cornstarch
    1 tablespoon butter or margarine

In small saucepan stir wine into catsup. Bring to boiling. Reduce heat; simmer, uncovered, 5 minutes. Blend together 2 tablespoons cold water and cornstarch; stir into wine mixture. Cook and stir till thickened and bubbly. Add butter; cook 1 minute more. Makes ¾ cup.

A FONDUE FIESTA

Mexican food and music go hand-in-hand, so combine the two with colorful south-of-the-border decorations for a wildly enthusiastic dinner. To an accompaniment of recorded trumpets, guitars, maracas, and castanets serve a snappy Mexi-Meatball Fondue, soft tortillas, and hot Mexican Chocolate.

MENU

Mexi-Meatball Fondue
Creamy Avocado Sauce   Mexican Hot Sauce
Chili-Cheese Sauce
Lettuce Wedges   Assorted Dressings
Soft Tortillas   Butter
Mexican Chocolate

Establish the mood with a colorful tabletop. Cut bright colored crepe paper into table runners, and add gaily decorated napkins inserted into napkin rings accented with crepe-paper flowers. Then place the fondue pot on an ornamental tray in the center and surround it with fondue plates and forks. Standard tableware of knives, forks, spoons, salad plates, and mugs should also be provided.

The fiesta atmosphere puts guests in a jovial mood, while a light work load makes this a festive occasion for hostess, too. In the morning, meatballs are shaped and sauces combined, then both refrigerated. About one to two hours before the party, meat is removed and allowed to reach room temperature. Sauces to be served warm are reheated at serving time. For the salad, lettuce is cut in wedges and an assortment of dressings offered in a server designed with individual compartments.

The soft tortillas, hot chocolate, and fondue require some last-minute attention. To make soft tortillas, the tortillas are not cooked but wrapped in foil and oven-heated till steamy. (To keep them hot at the table, stack on a plate; invert another plate on top.) Serve with butter and salt. Meanwhile, Mexican Chocolate with ingredients premeasured in saucepan and oil poured into the fondue cooker are heated.

Since ecstatic anticipation is sure to develop as these savory meatballs bubble vigorously, provide each diner with an extra fondue fork. One meatball can cook as another is taken out of the pot. Creamy Avocado Sauce, Mexican Hot Sauce, and Chili-Cheese Sauce are served with Mexi-Meatball Fondue.

MEXI-MEATBALL FONDUE

Combine ¾ cup soft bread crumbs (about 1 slice), ¼ cup chili sauce, 1 beaten egg, ½ teaspoon salt, ½ teaspoon instant minced onion, and ⅛ teaspoon garlic powder. Add ¾ pound ground beef and mix thoroughly. Shape mixture into about 30 meatballs.

Pour salad oil into fondue cooker to no more than ½ capacity or to depth of 2 inches. Heat over range to 375°. Add 1 teaspoon salt. Transfer cooker to fondue burner. Have meatballs at room temperature in serving bowl. Spear meatball with fondue fork; fry in hot oil for 1 to 2 minutes, or till desired doneness. Transfer hot meatball to dinner fork and dip in desired sauce. Makes 3 or 4 servings.

MEXICAN CHOCOLATE

Gets a foamy crown when beaten—

4 cups milk
5 1-ounce squares semisweet chocolate
6 inches stick cinnamon
1 teaspoon vanilla

Combine milk, semisweet chocolate, and cinnamon sticks in saucepan. Cook, stirring constantly, just till chocolate melts. Remove mixture from heat; remove cinnamon sticks and stir in vanilla. Beat mixture with rotary beater till frothy. Serve in warmed mugs with cinnamon stick stirrers, if desired. Makes 4 cups.

DINNER ORIENTAL-STYLE

Bring the land of silk, spices, and tea into your home with a meal featuring Chinese Hot Pot cooked in a Mongolian cooker. Bowls of steaming rice, a simple dessert, and plenty of hot tea accompany the main dish.

MENU

Chinese Hot Pot
Hot Cooked Rice
Orange Sherbet
Fortune Cookies
Hot Tea

To create this exotic mood, set the table with a bright red cloth, rich gold napkins, and a tiny spider mum at each plate. Then add chopsticks. (Include forks for the less-adventuresome.) Include a low table and sitting pillows to enhance that Far Eastern look, and light an incense burner to delicately scent the atmosphere before the dinner guests arrive.

To keep last minute fuss at a minimum, scoop the sherbet into serving dishes then freeze, make the sauces, and slice the meats and vegetables early in the day. Artfully arrange the uncooked meats and vegetables on a large serving platter. Cover with plastic wrap and refrigerate until an hour or two before dinner. About a half hour before serving, prepare the fluffy rice, allowing generous servings for all. Hot tea steeps to perfection in an oriental teapot as the evening's cooking adventure begins.

If using a charcoal Mongolian cooker, choose a well-ventilated eating area, preferably outdoors. To light the cooker, fill the chimney with charcoal; add charcoal starter. Cover the cooker, then light charcoal. Fill the cooking container with boiling broth and return to a simmer. Each guest then chooses what he wants from the assortment of meats and vegetables and cooks it in the bubbling broth.

When the meats and vegetables are all cooked, traditionalists poach eggs in the subtly flavored broth. To end the main course, add a little dry sherry to the cooking broth and serve it in oriental no-handle teacups.

As sherbet and fortune cookies are served for dessert, guests discuss their fortunes in the closing moments of this captivating meal.

CHINESE HOT POT

3/4 **pound large shrimp, peeled and cleaned (about 12 shrimp)**
2 **medium chicken breasts, skinned, boned, and very thinly sliced across grain**
1/2 **pound beef sirloin, very thinly sliced across grain**
1/2 **head Chinese cabbage *or* 1 head lettuce heart, coarsely cubed**
1 **cup cubed eggplant *or* 1 5-ounce can water chestnuts, drained and thinly sliced**
1 1/2 **cups halved fresh mushrooms**
4 **cups torn fresh spinach leaves with stems removed**

• • •

6 **13 3/4-ounce cans *or* 2 46-ounce cans chicken broth (10 1/2 cups) (not condensed)***
1 **tablespoon grated gingerroot *or* 1 teaspoon ground ginger***

At serving time, have uncooked meats and vegetables on large tray or platter and spinach in serving bowl at room temperature. Provide chopsticks, bamboo tongs, fondue forks, or wire ladles as cooking tools for guests.

In a fondue cooker*, electric skillet, chafing dish, or Mongolian cooker, heat chicken broth and ginger to a gentle boil. Pick up desired food; drop in bubbling broth. When cooked, lift out and dip in sauce. (Add more broth if needed.) Makes 6 servings.

*For fondue cooker, use two 13 3/4-ounce cans chicken broth and 1 teaspoon grated gingerroot *or* 1/4 teaspoon ground ginger.

Suggested sauces: Chinese Hot Mustard, Red Sauce, Ginger Soy, Peanut Sauce.

← **Fondue takes on an oriental flair** when Chinese Hot Pot with hot and spicy sauces is served. A fondue cooker, chafing dish, or electric skillet are equally as effective as the Mongolian cooker used here.

DIPPING INTO THE CHEESE POT

Originally a natural Swiss cheese melted in dry white wine, cheese fondue is an ingenious Swiss concoction. This elegant dish has many uses. It can introduce a multi-course meal of meat, vegetable, bread, salad, and dessert, or, stand as a main dish itself, by the addition of simple accompaniments, like relishes or salads, a beverage, and a light dessert.

With the easily mastered techniques of simmering and continual stirring, cheese fondue is prepared right before serving. Wine and lemon juice are warmed in a heavy saucepan just below boiling. Vigorous and constant stirring begins when the shredded cheeses, coated with cornstarch, are added, a handful at a time. Apply enough heat to melt the cheeses, but not enough to boil them. All is not lost should separation occur. To re-blend a separated mixture, combine 1 tablespoon cornstarch with 2 tablespoons wine and stir into the fondue.

The cheese-wine mixture is quickly transferred to fondue pot. Ceramic pots, similar to traditional Swiss caquelons, and metal cookers make equally suitable containers. Keep the cheese bubbly over the fondue burner—not too hot or it will become stringy nor too cool or it will become tough. If the fondue thickens during the meal, preheat a little more wine and add to the fondue, stirring briskly.

Each person spears a bread cube, piercing through the crust last. With a figure-8 motion, he swirls then withdraws the cheese-coated bread to eat. Thus, as the diners continue to dip, the fondue is kept in constant motion.

Whoops—who dropped a bread cube in the fondue? He must give a kiss to the friend of his choice. For the person who never lost a bread cube, there's another certain prize, the crusty cheese in the bottom of the pot.

CLASSIC CHEESE FONDUE

Combine 12 ounces *natural* Swiss cheese, shredded (3 cups), and 4 ounces *natural or process* Gruyere cheese, shredded (1 cup), with 1½ teaspoons cornstarch. Rub inside of heavy saucepan with 1 clove garlic, halved; discard garlic. Pour in 1 cup sauterne and 1 tablespoon lemon juice. Warm till air bubbles rise and cover surface. (Do not cover or allow to boil.)

Remember to stir vigorously and constantly from now on. Add a handful of cheeses, keeping heat medium (but do not boil). When melted, toss in another handful. After cheese is blended and bubbling and while still stirring, add dash ground nutmeg and dash pepper.

Quickly transfer to fondue pot; keep warm over fondue burner. (If fondue becomes too thick, add a little *warmed* sauterne.) Spear bread cube with fondue fork piercing crust last. Dip bread into fondue and swirl to coat bread. The swirling is important to keep fondue in motion. Makes 4 to 6 servings.

Suggested dippers: French bread, hard rolls, Italian bread, boiled potatoes.

CHEESE FONDUE DIPPERS

All dippers should be bite-sized. Cut bread cubes so that each has one crust. To estimate how many dippers are needed, consider appetites and accompanying dishes. Generally, 1 large loaf of French bread serves 6 to 8. Cooked meat and vegetable dippers are best served warm; raw vegetables best at room temperature.

French bread, hard rolls, Italian bread, bread sticks, toasted rye or whole wheat bread, English muffins
Cooked shrimp, chicken, or ham
Cherry tomatoes, cooked artichokes, carrot slices, cooked mushrooms, celery or green pepper pieces, fried potato nuggets, french-fried potatoes, boiled potatoes

---

A crunchy morsel of French bread is liberally → swirled in Classic Cheese Fondue. Glasses of chilled dry white wine make an excellent accompaniment beverage for this sophisticated cheese-wine dish.

CRAB-CHEESE FONDUE

>   8 ounces process American cheese,
>   shredded (2 cups)
>   8 ounces *natural* Cheddar cheese,
>   shredded (2 cups)
>   ¾ cup milk
>   2 teaspoons lemon juice
>   1 7½-ounce can crab meat, drained,
>   flaked, and cartilage removed

In saucepan slowly heat and stir cheeses and milk till melted. Stir in lemon juice. Add crab; heat. Transfer to fondue pot; place over fondue burner. Spear dipper on fondue fork; dip in fondue, swirling to coat. Serves 8 to 10.

Suggested dippers: French bread, cherry tomatoes, cooked artichokes.

BUTTERMILK FONDUE

>   2 tablespoons cornstarch
>   Dash ground nutmeg
>   1 pound *natural* Swiss cheese,
>   shredded (4 cups)
>   2 cups buttermilk

In mixing bowl combine cornstarch, ½ teaspoon salt, nutmeg, and dash pepper. Toss Swiss cheese with cornstarch mixture.

In saucepan carefully heat buttermilk. When warm, gradually add cheese; stir constantly till cheese melts and mixture thickens. Transfer to fondue pot; place over fondue burner. Spear dipper with fondue fork; dip in fondue, swirling to coat. Makes 6 to 8 servings.

Suggested dippers: French bread, English muffins, hard rolls.

CARAWAY-CHEESE FONDUE

In saucepan heat 1½ cups tomato juice and 2 teaspoons caraway seed but do not allow to boil. Toss 2 tablespoons all-purpose flour with 1 pound *natural* sharp Cheddar cheese, shredded (4 cups). Slowly add to juice, stirring constantly, till cheese melts and sauce is smooth.

Stir in ¼ cup milk and ½ teaspoon Worcestershire sauce. Pour into fondue pot; place over fondue burner. Spear dipper with fondue fork; swirl in fondue. Serves 6 to 8.

Suggested dippers: French bread, rye bread.

COTTAGE SWISS FONDUE

Mustard adds zesty background flavor—

>   2 tablespoons butter or margarine
>   2 tablespoons all-purpose flour
>   Dash garlic powder
>   1 teaspoon prepared mustard
>   1¼ cups milk
>   1 8-ounce carton cream-style
>   cottage cheese (1 cup)
>   8 ounces *natural* Swiss cheese,
>   shredded (2 cups)

In medium saucepan melt butter; blend in flour and garlic powder, then mustard. Add milk all at once. Cook quickly, stirring constantly, till thickened and bubbly. Add cottage cheese. Beat smooth with electric mixer or in blender.

Over medium heat gradually add Swiss cheese, stirring till cheese is melted. Pour into fondue pot; place over fondue burner. Spear dipper with fondue fork; dip in fondue, swirling to coat. (If mixture thickens upon standing, add a little milk.) Makes 4 to 6 servings.

Suggested dippers: French bread, fried potato nuggets, french-fried potatoes.

FONDUE, RAREBIT-STYLE

Good with toasted breads—

>   1½ cups sauterne
>   ½ cup water
>   2 tablespoons snipped chives
>   1 pound process American cheese,
>   shredded (4 cups)
>   2 tablespoons all-purpose flour
>   4 beaten egg yolks
>   ¼ teaspoon ground nutmeg

In saucepan heat wine, water, and chives. Coat cheese with flour. Add slowly to hot wine, stirring constantly till cheese melts and mixture is thickened and bubbly.

Stir a moderate amount of hot cheese mixture into egg yolks. Return to saucepan; cook and stir over low heat 2 minutes more. Add nutmeg. Pour into fondue pot; place over fondue burner. Spear dipper with fondue fork; dip in fondue, swirling to coat. Makes 6 to 8 servings.

Suggested dippers: French bread, cherry tomatoes, mushrooms.

BEER CHEESE FONDUE

    1 small clove garlic, halved
    ¾ cup beer
    8 ounces process Swiss cheese,
        shredded (2 cups)
    4 ounces sharp *natural* Cheddar
        cheese, shredded (1 cup)
    1 tablespoon all-purpose flour
        Dash bottled hot pepper sauce

Rub inside of heavy saucepan with cut surface of garlic; discard garlic. Add beer and heat slowly. Coat cheeses with flour. Gradually add to beer, stirring constantly, till mixture is thickened and bubbly. (Do not allow mixture to become too hot.) Stir in hot pepper sauce.

    Transfer to fondue pot; place over fondue burner. Spear dipper with fondue fork; dip into fondue, swirling to coat. (If mixture becomes too thick, stir in a little additional *warmed* beer.) Makes 4 to 6 servings.

    Suggested dippers: French bread, warm boiled potatoes.

In traditional cheese fondue recipes, the wine is heated in a saucepan but not allowed to boil. Then cheese is added, a handful at a time. Vigorous stirring blends the cheese-wine mixture together.

CREAMY PARMESAN FONDUE

    1½ cups milk
    2 8-ounce packages cream cheese,
        softened
    ½ teaspoon garlic salt
    1 2½-ounce container shredded
        Parmesan cheese (about ¾ cup)

With electric mixer add milk to cream cheese, mixing till well blended. Heat slowly in saucepan; add ½ teaspoon salt and garlic salt. Slowly add Parmesan, stirring till smooth.

    Pour into fondue pot; place over fondue burner. Spear dipper with fondue fork; dip in fondue, swirling to coat. (If mixture becomes too thick, stir in a little milk.) Serves 8 to 10.

    Suggested dippers: Bread sticks, warm cooked turkey or chicken.

CHEESE-SOUR CREAM FONDUE

    6 slices bacon
    ¼ cup minced onion
    2 teaspoons all-purpose flour
    1 pound sharp process American
        cheese, shredded (4 cups)
    2 cups dairy sour cream
    1 teaspoon Worcestershire sauce

In saucepan fry bacon till crisp; drain, reserving 1 tablespoon drippings. Crumble bacon; set aside. Cook onions in reserved drippings till tender but not brown. Stir in flour. Add remaining ingredients. Cook over low heat, stirring constantly, till cheese is melted.

    Pour into fondue pot. Top with bacon. Place over fondue burner. Spear dipper with fondue fork; dip into fondue. Makes 6 to 8 servings.

    Suggested dippers: Hard rolls, rye bread, mushrooms.

QUICK FONDUE

Mix two 10½-ounce cans condensed Cheddar cheese soup, ⅓ cup dry white wine, and few drops Worcestershire sauce in saucepan; heat. Pour into fondue pot; place over fondue burner. Spear dipper with fondue fork; dip into fondue, swirling to coat. Makes 4 to 6 servings.

    Suggested dippers: French bread, warm cooked shrimp, celery.

THE AFTER-SKI SCENE

Br-r-r-r, it's cold outside—so build a roaring blaze in the fireplace, bring on the fondue, and start swapping skiing tales. If you're not in ski country, plan this "warm-up" party to follow some other winter activity.

MENU

Fondue Italiano
Green Salad Ensemble
Pineapple Delight Cake
Beer
Coffee

Skiing parties are fun, and often you end up with more people than you set out with. So have extra food on hand to take care of new-found friends on the slopes. This sharing atmosphere will make all guests feel welcome.

Since everyone will want to participate in the skiing, prepare most of the food ahead and store properly till serving time. Early in the day, bake the cake, prepare the salad minus the dressing, and cube the bread. Start Fondue Italiano by browning the ground beef; mix in spaghetti sauce mix and tomato sauce. When it's time to eat, it will take only a few minutes to complete the final recipe steps.

Hungry skiers will be anxious to eat, so make the table setting simple and quick to arrange. Simple, however, needn't mean dull. Co-ordinated napkins and table runners or table-cloth with informal plates and beer mugs build a delightful mood. The attractive fondue container becomes a centerpiece as well as the serving dish. Complete the setting with bread basket, individual salad bowls, cake platter, fondue forks, and coffee cups.

Fondue and friends make a gay after-ski party. Fondue Italiano, tossed salad, and mugs of cold beer are ready in a jiffy to feed the famished skiers. Good food and conversation soon shut out the cold weather.

FONDUE ITALIANO

½ pound ground beef
½ envelope spaghetti sauce mix
1 15-ounce can tomato sauce
12 ounces *natural* Cheddar cheese, shredded (3 cups)
4 ounces *natural* Mozzarella cheese, shredded (1 cup)
1 tablespoon cornstarch
½ cup chianti

. . .

Italian bread, cut in bite-size pieces, each with one crust

In saucepan brown ground beef; drain off excess fat. Stir in spaghetti sauce mix and tomato sauce. Add cheeses gradually; stir over low heat till cheese is melted. Blend together cornstarch and wine; add to cheese mixture. Cook and stir till thickened and bubbly.

Transfer to fondue pot; place over fondue burner. Spear bread cube with fondue fork; dip in fondue mixture, swirling to coat. (If fondue becomes thick, add a little *warmed* chianti.) Makes about 6 servings.

GREEN SALAD ENSEMBLE

Place 2 cups torn lettuce and 2 cups torn curly endive in salad bowl. On top arrange 2 medium tomatoes, cut in wedges; ½ medium green pepper, sliced; ½ cup sliced celery; ¼ cup sliced radishes; ¼ cup onion rings. Serve with French-style dressing. Makes 6 servings.

PINEAPPLE DELIGHT CAKE

Prepare one package 1-layer-size yellow cake mix according to package directions. Bake in greased and lightly floured 8x1½-inch round pan at 350° for 25 minutes or till done. Cool. Split to form 2 layers.

Spread *half* of one 22-ounce can pineapple pie filling on bottom layer; replace top layer. Spread remaining pie filling on top of cake to within ½-inch of edge. Beat 3 egg whites to soft peaks; gradually add 6 tablespoons sugar, beating to stiff peaks. Spread over top and sides of cake. Sprinkle 2 tablespoons flaked coconut over top. Bake at 350° for 10 minutes or till lightly browned. Cool.

WINE GUIDE

Wines can be classified in five groups by their common characteristics. This chart lists some wines in each group and tells how to serve them with cooked-at-the-table dishes. Although pairing of foods and wines should ultimately be based on personal preference, foods most suited to each group are indicated.

Selection of the appropriate wine should be coupled with proper serving techniques. Here are some general serving tips that are good guidelines to follow. Sweet wines should not be served with main dishes; neither should red wines be served with fish. Uncork red wines an hour ahead to develop full flavor.

Group	Foods Served with Group	Wine Types to Serve
Appetizer Wines (Serve at room temperature, 60° to 70°, or chilled, 40° to 45°.)	Alone as an appetizer or with all appetizer foods	Sherry, especially dry varieties Vermouth, both dry and sweet Flavored Wines
Red Table Wines (Serve at room temperature, 60° to 70° *except* for Rosé.) (Serve chilled, 45° to 50°.)	All red meats including steaks, veal; game, goose, duck, turkey; cheese	Burgundy (Pinot Noir) Beaujolais (Gamay) Red Chianti (Barbera) Claret (Cabernet Sauvignon) Rosé
White Table Wines (Serve chilled, 45° to 50°.)	All poultry, chicken, turkey; fish, shellfish; veal; cheese dishes The traditional Swiss wines served with cheese fondue	Rhine (Riesling) Sauterne, drier varieties (Semillon, Sauvignon Blanc) Chablis Moselle White Burgundy (Pinot Chardonnay) Neuchatel, Dézaley, Fendant de Sion
Dessert Wines (Serve at room temperature, 60° to 70°.)	Alone as after-dinner wine or with fruit, nuts, cakes, some dessert cheeses	Port, Ruby or Tawny Muscatel White Tokay Sherry, Sweet or Cream Sweet Madeira Sauterne, sweeter varieties
Sparkling Wines (Serve chilled, 40° to 45°.)	Most types of foods	Champagne—very dry (brut), semi-dry (sec), less dry (demi-sec), or sweet (doux) Sparkling Burgundy Sparkling Rosé

WINES TO USE IN CHEESE FONDUE

Cheese fondue recipes using wine as an ingredient usually specify a dry white wine, the most traditional being the Swiss wine, Neuchatel. Those listed below may be used interchangeably in Classic Cheese Fondue (see page 26). Several types listed include wines with colors and flavors other than those described here. Wines with the characteristics indicated, however, are best suited for cheese fondue.

When Cheese Fondue Used as	Use This Wine Type	With These Characteristics
Appetizer	Sherry	Very dry to dry, pale amber, nutty flavor
Appetizer or Main Dish	Champagne	Dry (brut, sec, or demi-sec), pale gold, fruit flavor
	Neuchatel	Dry, pale gold, light-bodied, lively, crisp
	Fendant de Sion	Dry, pale gold, lively, crisp
Main Dish	Rhine	Dry, pale gold to slightly green-gold, light-bodied, tart
	Moselle	Dry, pale, light-bodied
	Chablis	Very dry, pale gold, fruit flavor
	Sauterne	Dry, golden, full-bodied, fragrant

CLASSIC CHEESE FONDUE VARIATIONS

Cheeses vary considerably in appearance, texture, and flavor. In this respect, they are very individualistic. One cheese cannot be substituted at random for another in a cooked cheese dish.

Traditionally, cheese fondue recipes use a well-aged natural Swiss (Emmenthal) cheese or a blend of Swiss cheese and Gruyere. Nevertheless, processed forms of these cheeses are also suitable. To give interesting flavor variation to your cheese fondue, the other natural cheeses listed below (most are not available in a processed form) can be substituted for the Swiss cheese in Classic Cheese Fondue (see page 26). Use *12 ounces (3 cups shredded)* of one of these cheeses. Adjust wine and lemon juice levels as indicated in the columns adjacent to each cheese, then continue preparing the cheese fondue following the Classic Cheese Fondue method.

Note: Several other cheeses tested produced mixtures that separated into two layers of wine and cheese, or were too runny in the proportions established in the Classic Cheese Fondue recipe. These include Gouda, Mozzarella, Provolone, and Stilton. This is not to say they cannot be used for cheese fondue, but proportions must be carefully adjusted. Several of these tested cheese fondue variations will be found elsewhere in this book.

Natural Cheese	Wine	Lemon Juice	Flavor of Cheese
Brick	1 cup	1 tablespoon	Mild to moderately sharp; midway between Cheddar and Limburger
Colby	¾ cup	2 teaspoons	Mild to mellow; similar to Cheddar
Fontina	1 cup	1 tablespoon	Delicate, nutty flavor
Monterey Jack	¾ cup	2 teaspoons	Mild
Muenster	1 cup	1 tablespoon	Mild to mellow

FONDUE MEAL CAPPERS

A warm chocolate sauce in which pieces of cake or fruit are dipped, Chocolate Fondue, is the classic dessert fondue. Originated for the promotion of Swiss chocolate, Chocolate Fondue soon sparked ideas for a variety of dessert fondues including other warm dessert sauces and deep-fat fried desserts.

Dessert fondue sets, which usually include a stand with candle warmer and a small ceramic or metal fondue pot, are available. Any metal pot, however, can be used for this type of fondue. Ceramic containers can also be used for fondues that do not require hot oil.

Dessert fondues are used as either a final course or as an in-between-meal refreshment. Since most dessert fondues are rich, they are best served and enjoyed with a beverage after a light meal. One or two dessert fondues, an assortment of dippers, and a beverage make a delicious refreshment suitable for an afternoon bridge club, a small party with friends, or an after-theater get-together.

Most of the dessert fondue is prepared before serving time. Fondues that involve deep-fat frying can be prepared up to the point of frying and dippers can be cut into bite-size pieces. Store each item appropriately to maintain high quality. Shortly before serving time, heat oil over the range, or prepare sauce-type fondues in saucepan and then transfer to fondue pot. Keep sauces over low heat so they are warm but not hot enough to burn the mouth. At the table, each person fries his dessert in hot oil or dips it in the warm sauce.

CHOCOLATE FONDUE

>   6 1-ounce squares unsweetened
>   chocolate
> 1½ cups sugar
>   1 cup light cream
> ½ cup butter or margarine
> ⅛ teaspoon salt
>   3 tablespoons crème de cacao or
>   orange-flavored liqueur

In saucepan melt chocolate over low heat. Add sugar, cream, butter, and salt. Cook, stirring constantly, about 5 minutes or till thickened. Stir in liqueur. Pour into fondue pot; place over fondue burner. Spear dipper with fondue fork; dip in sauce. Makes 6 to 8 servings.

Suggested dippers: Angel cake, pound cake, apples, maraschino cherries, marshmallows.

DESSERT FONDUE DIPPERS

All dippers should be in bite-size pieces and at room temperature. Allow 8 to 12 pieces per serving. Drain canned or frozen fruits thoroughly. *To keep fresh fruit bright, dip in ascorbic acid color keeper or lemon juice mixed with a little water.

Cherries, strawberries, bananas*, apples*, seedless grapes, pears*, pineapple, oranges, mandarin oranges, melons, peaches*, maraschino cherries, dates.

Angel, sponge, chiffon, or pound cake, doughnuts, brownies, cookies.

Marshmallows, large salted nuts, large puffy popcorn kernels, pretzels.

CHOCOLATE-NUT FONDUE

In saucepan combine one 6-ounce package semisweet chocolate pieces, ½ cup sugar, and ½ cup milk. Cook, stirring constantly, till chocolate is melted. Add ½ cup chunk-style peanut butter; mix well. Pour into fondue pot; place over fondue burner. Spear dipper with fondue fork; dip in sauce. Serves 6 to 8.

Suggested dippers: Bananas, apples, pound cake, angel cake, marshmallows.

Rich and velvety Chocolate Fondue provides a →
sweet ending for a special meal. Pour warm sauce in fondue pot just before serving; keep warm over low heat or candle. Pass fruit or cake dippers.

CREAMY RASPBERRY FONDUE

      1 4–ounce container whipped cream
         cheese
      2 10–ounce packages frozen
         raspberries, thawed
   1/4 cup cornstarch
      2 tablespoons sugar
   1/4 cup brandy

Let cream cheese come to room temperature. In saucepan crush raspberries slightly. Blend together cornstarch and 1/2 cup cold water; add to berries. Cook and stir till thickened and bubbly. Sieve; discard seeds. Pour into fondue pot; place over fondue burner. Add cream cheese, stirring till melted. Stir in sugar; gradually add brandy. Spear fruit or cake cube with fondue fork; dip in fondue. Makes 6 servings.

Suggested dippers: Pound cake, pears, peaches.

PEPPERMINT FONDUE

In saucepan heat 1/2 cup milk and 3 tablespoons butter or margarine till butter is melted. Add one 14-ounce package creamy-white frosting mix and 3/4 cup finely crushed peppermint candies; mix well. Stir in 2 drops red food coloring. Pour into fondue pot; place over fondue burner. Dip cookies or cake in fondue. Serves 6.

Suggested dippers: Chocolate wafers, pound cake, angel cake.

BUTTERSCOTCH FONDUE

   1/2 cup butter or margarine
      2 cups brown sugar
      1 cup light corn syrup
      1 15–ounce can sweetened
         condensed milk (1 1/3 cups)
      1 teaspoon vanilla

In saucepan melt butter; stir in sugar, corn syrup, and 2 tablespoons water. Bring to boiling. Stir in milk; simmer, stirring constantly, till mixture reaches thread stage (230°). Add vanilla. Pour into fondue pot; place over fondue burner. Spear dipper with fondue fork; dip in fondue. (If mixture becomes too thick, stir in a little milk or water.) Makes 8 servings.

Suggested dippers: Pound cake, vanilla wafers, apples, popcorn.

CARAMEL FONDUE

Combine one 14-ounce package vanilla caramels and 1/3 cup water in top of double boiler; melt over hot water, stirring frequently. Add dash salt. Pour sauce into fondue pot; place over fondue burner. (If mixture is too thick, stir in a little water.) Spear dipper with fondue fork; dip in fondue. Makes 4 servings.

Suggested dippers: Apples, bananas, peaches, marshmallows.

FRIED CREAM SQUARES

Ladyfingers are sandwiched between cream—

   1/2 cup sugar
   1/2 cup cornstarch
      2 cups light cream
   1/2 cup milk
      3 slightly beaten egg yolks
         Few drops vanilla
         Few drops almond extract
      1 3–ounce package ladyfingers (8),
         split in half lengthwise
      2 beaten eggs
   1 1/2 cups ground almonds
   1/4 cup fine dry bread crumbs
         Salad oil

Line bottom and sides of 9x9x2-inch pan with foil. In saucepan combine sugar, cornstarch, and dash salt. Stir in cream and milk. Cook over medium heat, stirring constantly, till mixture is thickened and bubbly. Stir small amount of hot mixture into egg yolks. Return to hot mixture; cook and stir 2 minutes. Remove from heat; add vanilla and almond extract.

Spread *half* the pudding mixture in foil-lined pan. Arrange ladyfingers evenly over pudding; top with remaining pudding. Cool; cover and chill thoroughly several hours or overnight.

Turn out onto waxed paper. Remove foil and cut into 1-inch squares. Dip squares into beaten eggs; coat with mixture of nuts and bread crumbs. Chill, uncovered, about 1 hour.

Pour salad oil into fondue cooker to no more than 1/2 capacity or to depth of 2 inches. Heat over range to 400°. Add 1 teaspoon salt. Transfer to fondue burner. Spear dessert square through cake layer with fondue fork; fry in hot oil a few seconds till browned. Transfer to dinner fork before eating. Serves 14 to 16.

FRENCH-TOASTED FONDUE

Cut French bread into about 50 bite-size pieces, each with one crust. Combine 2 well-beaten eggs, ½ cup milk, and ¼ teaspoon salt.

Pour salad oil into fondue cooker to no more than ½ capacity or to depth of 2 inches. Heat over range to 375°. Add 1 teaspoon salt. Transfer cooker to fondue burner. Spear bread through crust with fondue fork; dip in egg mixture, letting excess drip off. Fry in hot oil till golden brown. Transfer to dinner fork; dip in Fluffy Maple Sauce. Makes 6 to 8 servings.

Fluffy Maple Sauce: Thoroughly cream together 1½ cups sifted confectioners' sugar, ½ cup butter or margarine, ½ cup maple-flavored syrup, and 1 egg yolk. Fold in 1 stiffly beaten egg white. Chill. Makes 2 cups.

ICE CREAM-AND-CAKE CUBES

Ice cream is the surprise filling—

    1 slice neopolitan ice cream
    1 12-ounce loaf pound cake
    2 beaten eggs
    ½ cup milk
    ¼ teaspoon salt
      Salad oil

Cut ice cream into eight 1-inch cubes; freeze till hard. Meanwhile, cut pound cake into eight 1½-inch cubes. To hollow out centers, use sharp knife to make a horizontal slit ¼-inch from bottom of each cake cube to within ¼-inch of the other sides. Leaving ¼-inch around all sides, cut a square straight down from top of cube to slit. Carefully lift out. (This leaves a piece of cake with ¼-inch-thick sides and bottom, and a hollow in the middle.)

Insert an ice cream cube in each hollow. Close top of ice cream-filled-hollow with small piece of cake. Freeze cake cubes till needed. Just before serving combine eggs, milk, and salt. Pour into small serving bowl.

Pour salad oil into fondue cooker to no more than ½ capacity or to depth of 2 inches. Heat over range to 400°. Add 1 teaspoon salt. Transfer cooker to fondue burner. Spear a solidly frozen cake cube with fondue fork; dip in egg mixture, turning to coat all sides. Fry in hot oil a few seconds till golden brown. Transfer to dinner fork before eating. Makes 4 servings.

FRUIT FRITTERS

Served with a tangy orange-lemon sauce—

    2 tablespoons orange juice
    1 tablespoon sugar
    2 *firm* bananas
    1 medium eating apple
    1 small fresh pineapple
    1 4-ounce jar maraschino cherries
    1 cup sifted all-purpose flour
    ½ teaspoon baking powder
    ⅔ cup milk
    1 slightly beaten egg
    2 tablespoons butter or margarine,
        melted
    ¼ teaspoon lemon extract
            • • •
    ½ cup sugar
    2 tablespoons cornstarch
    ¾ cup water
    ½ teaspoon grated orange peel
    ¼ cup orange juice
    2 tablespoons butter or margarine
    ¼ teaspoon grated lemon peel
    1 tablespoon lemon juice
      Salad oil

Combine the 2 tablespoons orange juice and 1 tablespoon sugar. Cut bananas, apple, and pineapple in bite-size pieces. Let stand in orange juice-sugar mixture till needed. Thoroughly drain maraschino cherries.

Sift together flour, baking powder, and ½ teaspoon salt. Combine milk, egg, melted butter or margarine, and lemon extract; add to flour mixture, beating till smooth.

Prepare sauce by combining the ½ cup sugar, cornstarch, and dash salt in small saucepan. Stir in water. Cook, stirring constantly, till thickened and bubbly; continue cooking 3 minutes more. Remove from heat; stir in orange peel, the ¼ cup orange juice, the remaining butter, lemon peel and juice. Keep warm.

Pour salad oil into fondue cooker to no more than ½ capacity or to depth of 2 inches. Heat over range to 375°. Add 1 teaspoon salt. Transfer cooker to fondue burner. Have *well-drained* bananas, apples, pineapple, and maraschino cherries at room temperature in serving bowls.

Spear fruit piece with fondue fork; dip in egg-flour batter. Fry in hot oil 2 to 3 minutes or till golden brown. Transfer to dinner fork; dip in warm sauce. Makes 6 to 8 servings.

DINNER ON THE MOVE

Fondue pots are laden with enjoyment at a progressive dinner finale. Volunteer to be dessert hostess and serve Mini Pastries au Fondue.

MENU

Spicy Appetizer Meatballs
Toss-Your-Own-Salad
Oven-Fried Chicken
Mini Pastries au Fondue
Coffee or Tea

The refreshing aspect of a progressive dinner is that no one person prepares the entire meal. The first way to get the party going right is to coordinate the menu with the hostesses who are preparing and serving each course. This gives rise to a colorful menu. The foods served should hold well and not require many last-minute finishing touches so hosts and hostesses can relax while they, as diners, gather at someone else's home.

Final details for the other courses are completed by the co-hostesses while you concentrate on dessert. Since everyone cooks his own pastries in hot oil, provide a card table with chairs and one fondue cooker for every four persons. Borrow or rent any of these you need, making certain enough fondue forks are included as well. Other equipment needs are minimal: dessert plates and forks, napkins, condiment bowls for each table, and cups and spoons for beverage. There are no centerpieces to fuss over with fondue in the limelight.

Early on the party day, card tables and place settings can be arranged. Tables should be placed with space enough for easy movement yet close enough for inter-table talk. Wrap dough around fruits and candies for the pastries and refrigerate till dinner begins.

When the meal-marchers arrive, just heat the oil in fondue cookers. Each diner spears a pastry, cooks it in the hot oil, then dips it in one of the sugar condiments. It's a top-notch end to lively house-hopping.

SPICY APPETIZER MEATBALLS

Combine ¼ cup fine dry bread crumbs, 1 slightly beaten egg, 1 teaspoon prepared mustard, ½ teaspoon salt, and ⅛ teaspoon pepper. Add ¾ pound ground beef and one 4¾-ounce can liver spread; mix well. Shape into 1-inch meatballs, using round teaspoon meat mixture for each. Cover tightly; refrigerate overnight.

Just before baking, roll meatballs in 2 cups corn chips, crushed (¾ cup). Bake on rack in shallow pan at 350° for 10 minutes. Turn; bake 10 minutes more. Makes about 60 meatballs.

MINI PASTRIES AU FONDUE

Fried puffs with bonuses inside—

> 1 **tube refrigerated crescent rolls (8 rolls)**
> **Miniature chocolate-covered cream mints**
> **Halved vanilla caramels**
> **Halved marshmallows**
> **Candied cherries *or* candied pineapple chunks**
> **Salad oil**
> **Sifted confectioners' sugar**
> ½ **cup granulated sugar**
> ½ **teaspoon ground cinnamon**

Separate roll dough into 4 rectangles; pinch together along perforations. Cut *each* rectangle into eight 2-inch squares. Place a piece of candy or fruit on each square. Fold corners of dough over candy to cover completely; seal edges well. Repeat for remaining squares.

Pour salad oil into fondue cooker to no more than ½ capacity or to depth of 2 inches. Heat over range to 375°. Add 1 teaspoon salt. Transfer to fondue burner. Have pastries at room temperature in serving bowl. Spear a pastry with fondue fork. Fry in hot oil till dark golden brown, about 2 to 2½ minutes. Dip in confectioners' sugar or granulated sugar-cinnamon mixture. Makes 32 pastries.

Mini Pastries au Fondue create excitement as → guests spear and cook surprise-filled pastries. Easy to make, squares of refrigerated crescent-roll dough are sealed around bite-size pieces of fruit or candy.

CHAFING DISH TREASURY

Long a symbol of cooking elegance, the chafing dish is a boon to today's busy hostess. It enables her to serve graciously with a minimum of effort. Although chafing dish-like utensils were found in the ruins of Pompeii, the chafing dish did not achieve its modern form until the nineteenth century. The glories of chafing dish cookery, which reached a popularity peak during the gay 1890's, have been rediscovered.

Fascinate guests and family alike with such classics as Crepes Suzette and Lobster Newburg as well as new hot dips, hearty main dishes, spectacular desserts, and steaming beverages.

If you are in the mood for a Self-Service Supper, Dinner by Candlelight, Show-Stopping Dinner, or Dinner on the Patio, this section offers complete menu and table decorating ideas.

This hearty Deutsch Dinner is quickly tossed together in a chafing dish. Knackwurst slices, potato cubes, and crumbled bacon are combined with the German-style dressing at the table.

A DISH WITH MANY USES

Ever dream of being a star? Even if your stage aspirations have long been forgotten, dust the cobwebs off that dream. Make your debut at your next dinner party by cooking at the table using a chafing dish. Chafing dish cookery not only caters to the showmanship in all of us, it also enables the hostess to spend her time with guests. They become the supporting players.

Conceivably with several chafing dishes and some delay between courses, you could serve a completely cooked-at-the-table meal of Onion-Wine Soup, Classic Beef Stroganoff, and Hot Fruit Medley. Practically though, it is better to concentrate on one chafing dish creation per meal. If you are a beginner, choose a simple recipe, then as you become more adept, try more involved dishes.

With practice and organization, you'll soon be ready to occupy center-stage of the dinner party. Rehearsing your technique before the performance is essential to create the impression of elegance with little effort. At the dress rehearsal before the family, simulate the final conditions as closely as possible.

Organization is the other essential part of your performance. When selecting the stage area, choose a section of the table that is strategically located, well lighted, and not in a direct draft. Besides the chafing dish set on a heat-proof tray or mat to catch spills, you will need an attractive serving tray to hold extra fuel, a small towel, stirring utensils (preferably wooden), and the ingredients to be added at the table. If the table is small, you may want to set the ingredients and other props nearby on a small table or serving cart.

All chopping and measuring should be done behind the scenes, being careful to chop pieces uniformly. Add eye-appeal to the finished dish with garnishes cut in decorative shapes. Put each ingredient in a separate container. (Dry seasonings or liquids may be combined beforehand but don't combine everything in one bowl as this ruins the show.) As chafing dish cookery becomes a frequent feature of your dinner parties, you may want to add a professional touch to the performance by purchasing small attractive containers to hold ingredients.

Cooking-at-the-table is the spectacular result of careful preparation, so as the curtain rises, bring the ingredient tray to the table and proceed with your guest-awing performance.

TYPES OF CHAFING DISHES

The term chafing dish, dating from at least the 15th century, has evolved to mean any utensil used over a burner to cook food at the table. Although handsome chafing dishes are available as a complete unit, you can improvise by using an attractive skillet or saucepan with one of the numerous portable burners.

The basic chafing dish unit consists of several parts as shown in the sketch at right. The main parts are the skillet-like blazer pan, bain-marie (hot water bath), burner, and cover which is used to steam foods.

The skillet-type blazer pan could be called the most important part of the chafing dish since it holds the food. Recipe directions will specify whether to use it over direct heat or over the water-filled bain-marie.

The bain-marie fits under the blazer pan and is designed to hold hot water for a double-boiler effect. The hot water acts as an insulator for heat sensitive foods or holds, at eating temperature, foods that are not served immediately. The bain-marie may be removable or permanently attached to the stand. When using the bain-marie, first set it in place on the stand, then fill about $\frac{1}{4}$ full with boiling water.

Ranging from simple to very ornate, chafing dishes are available in an assortment of materials and finishes including copper, brass, stainless steel, sterling silver, plain or color-coated aluminum, and pewter. Follow the manufacturer's directions for caring for the finish.

Chafing dish size also varies. Small ones are suitable for appetizers and rich dessert sauces, while larger ones are needed for main dishes. The number of people being served will also indicate what size chafing dish is needed.

Aside from the basic chafing dish this family includes optional accessories—skillet, crepes pan, buffet saucepan, and Dutch saucepan. The

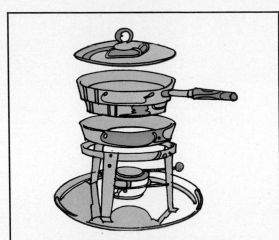

This basic chafing dish has six main parts—cover, blazer pan, bain-marie, stand, burner with flame adjuster, and heat-proof tray.

The scope of chafing dish cookery widens with optional accessories such as a crepes pan, skillet, buffet saucepan, and Dutch saucepan.

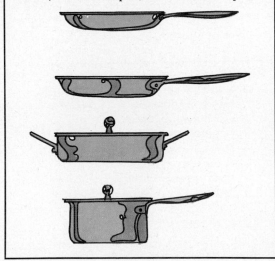

can be used for hot beverages or to keep foods warm. However, because of the large volume of food it will hold, a chafing dish burner will not supply sufficient heat to cook foods in this pan.

TYPES OF BURNERS

Fondue and chafing dish burners are classified by heat source—alcohol, canned heat, electricity, butane, or candle.

Alcohol burners, with a wick or with a pad of compressed fiber, use denatured (wood) alcohol as fuel. This type of alcohol, which can be purchased at drug or hardware stores, is poisonous so mark it as such and store it out of children's reach. Since this alcohol ruins wood finishes, always fill the burner over a newspaper-covered area. Fill the burner only half full and never refill while it is burning or still hot. After filling, wipe the outside with a dry cloth to catch all spills. Raise or lower the wick to regulate the flame of the wick-type burners. Burners with a compressed fiber pad are regulated by opening or closing the damper. To extinguish an alcohol burner, set the cover or snuffer in place. Because of the hazard of fire, always empty and thoroughly dry an alcohol burner before storing the chafing dish.

Canned heat units consist of a stand with a holder for the canned heat (solidified alcohol) container. These holders usually have a movable cover for heat regulation but the can lid may also be used. Close the cover or set the can lid in place to extinguish the flame.

Electric units have the advantage of a thermostatically-controlled heating unit with high to low temperature settings. Their mobility is limited only by the need for an electric outlet. These units should be operated and cleaned according to the manufacturers' directions.

Although butane burners do not come as part of a fondue or chafing dish set, they can be used in combination with an attractive saucepan or skillet in place of a chafing dish or fondue cooker. These burners burn butane gas which is available in small pressurized filling tubes. Fill and care for these butane burners by following the manufacturers' directions.

The final type of heat source is a small candle. Candle warmers are not designed for cooking but rather are suitable for keeping sauce-type dessert fondues or other foods warm on the dinner or buffet table.

chafing skillet is used over direct heat for dishes from main dish to dessert. The crepes pan, a smaller skillet with flared sides, is designed for frying the thin pancake-like crepes. However, since this is a time-consuming task, the crepes can be made ahead and then served, flaming or in a sauce, in this pan.

The buffet saucepan's added depth and surface area make it ideal for saucy dishes such as Newburgs or soups. The deep Dutch saucepan

APPETITE TEMPTERS

CRANBERRY-SAUCED BITES

1 cup sugar
½ pound fresh cranberries (2 cups)
¼ cup catsup
1 tablespoon lemon juice
Fully-cooked ham, chicken,
and turkey, cubed

In large saucepan combine sugar and 1 cup water; stir to dissolve sugar. Heat to boiling; boil 5 minutes. Add cranberries; cook till skins pop, about 5 minutes. Remove from heat. Stir in catsup and lemon juice. Pour into small blazer pan; place ham, chicken, and turkey cubes in sauce. Keep warm over hot water (bain-marie). Spear with cocktail picks. Makes 2 cups sauce.

DELRAY SHRIMP DIP

Next time scoop with rye melba toast—

1 10½-ounce can condensed
cream of shrimp soup
4 ounces sharp process American
cheese, shredded (1 cup)
1 4½-ounce can shrimp, drained and
cut up
2 tablespoons milk
¼ teaspoon bottled hot pepper sauce

In blazer pan of chafing dish combine all ingredients. Heat slowly over direct heat; stir till bubbly. Keep warm over hot water. Serve with melba toast. Makes 2¼ cups.

DEVILED CHEESE DIP

A deviled ham and cream cheese combo—

In blazer pan of chafing dish melt one 8-ounce package cream cheese slowly over direct heat, stirring constantly. Add one 4½-ounce can deviled ham, 3 tablespoons milk, 1 tablespoon finely chopped onion, and 1 tablespoon chopped canned pimiento; heat through. Keep warm over hot water. Serve with rich round crackers and crisp vegetables. Makes 1½ cups.

CHEESE-BACON DIP

1 8-ounce package cream cheese
8 ounces process American cheese,
shredded (2 cups)
½ cup milk
¼ teaspoon onion salt
¼ teaspoon dry mustard
3 drops bottled hot pepper sauce
• • •
6 slices bacon crisp-cooked
and crumbled

In blazer pan of small chafing dish melt cream cheese slowly over direct heat, stirring constantly. Add American cheese, milk, onion salt, mustard, and hot pepper sauce. Cook, stirring constantly, till cheeses melt. Add bacon. Keep warm over hot water. Serve with assorted crackers. (If mixture becomes too thick, stir in a little milk.) Makes about 1½ cups.

LOBSTER DIP ELEGANTE

1 8-ounce package cream cheese
¼ cup mayonnaise or salad dressing
1 clove garlic, crushed
1 teaspoon sugar
1 teaspoon prepared mustard
1 teaspoon grated onion
Dash seasoned salt
1 5-ounce can lobster, drained,
flaked, and cartilage removed
3 tablespoons sauterne

In blazer pan of small chafing dish melt cream cheese slowly over direct heat, stirring constantly. Blend in mayonnaise or salad dressing, garlic, sugar, mustard, onion, and salt. Stir in lobster and sauterne; heat through. Keep warm over hot water. Serve with melba toast and assorted crackers. Makes about 1¾ cups.

Add a splash of color to the buffet table with Cranberry-Sauced Bites, tender cubes of ham and turkey in a bright red cranberry sauce. It's not only lovely but also delicious. Serve with an appetizer wine. →

CRAB-CHEESE DIP

      2 tablespoons finely chopped onion
      2 tablespoons finely chopped
          green pepper
      2 tablespoons butter or margarine
      1 10½-ounce can condensed cream
          of mushroom soup
      ½ cup milk
      6 ounces *natural* Cheddar cheese,
          shredded (1½ cups)
      2 beaten eggs
      1 7½-ounce can crab meat, drained,
          flaked, and cartilage removed
        Dash ground nutmeg

In blazer pan of chafing dish cook onion and green pepper with butter over direct heat till tender but not brown. Stir in soup; gradually blend in milk. Cook and stir till bubbly.

Add cheese to soup mixture; heat and stir till melted. Stir a moderate amount of cheese mixture into beaten eggs; return to hot mixture. Cook and stir till bubbly. Add crab and nutmeg. Keep warm over hot water. Serve with assorted crackers. Makes about 3½ cups.

CREAMY CLAM DIP

Drain one 7½-ounce can minced clams, reserving 2 teaspoons juice. In blazer pan of small chafing dish melt one 8-ounce package cream cheese over direct heat, stirring constantly. Add clams; reserved juice; 1 clove garlic, crushed; 1½ teaspoons Worcestershire sauce; ½ teaspoon lemon juice; and ¼ teaspoon paprika.

Cook, stirring constantly, till mixture is blended and heated through. Keep warm over hot water. Serve with assorted crackers, chips, or celery sticks. Makes 1 cup.

CHILI CON CHEESE DIP

Pour one 15-ounce can chili with beans into blazer pan of chafing dish; mash beans with fork. Add one 10-ounce package frozen Welsh rarebit, 1 teaspoon Worcestershire sauce, ¼ teaspoon garlic powder, and few drops bottled hot pepper sauce. Cook over direct heat, stirring constantly, till blended and heated through. Keep warm over hot water. Serve with corn chips. Makes about 3 cups.

Crowd-pleasers like Chili Con Cheese Dip are always enthusiastically received. This convenient dip, made from canned chili and frozen Welsh rarebit, is blended in minutes when heated in a chafing dish.

DUO CHEESE DIP

      2 tablespoons butter or margarine
      3 tablespoons all-purpose flour
      1 teaspoon grated onion
      ¼ teaspoon bottled hot pepper sauce
        Dash freshly ground pepper
      1 beef bouillon cube
      1⅓ cups boiling water
              · · ·
      4 ounces process cheese spread,
          shredded (1 cup)
      4 ounces process Swiss cheese,
          shredded (1 cup)

In blazer pan of chafing dish melt butter over direct heat; blend in flour, onion, hot pepper sauce, and pepper. Dissolve bouillon cube in boiling water; add to flour mixture. Cook and stir till thickened and bubbly. Add cheeses; heat, stirring constantly, till melted. Keep warm over hot water. Serve with fully-cooked ham cubes, garlic bread sticks, rye melba toast, or rye crackers. Makes 2 cups.

ONION-CHEDDAR SOUP

In blazer pan of chafing dish cook 1 large onion, chopped (1 cup), in 3 tablespoons butter or margarine over direct heat till tender but not brown. Blend in 3 tablespoons all-purpose flour, 1/2 teaspoon salt, and dash pepper. Add 4 cups scalded milk all at once. Bring to boiling, stirring constantly. Remove from heat.

Add 8 ounces sharp process Cheddar cheese, shredded (2 cups), stirring till melted. Ladle into soup bowls. Garnish each serving with paprika and snipped chives. Serves 4 to 6.

ONION-WINE SOUP

  3 medium onions, thinly sliced
      (2 cups)
  1/4 cup butter or margarine
  2 101/2-ounce cans *condensed*
      chicken broth
  1/2 cup dry white wine
  6 French bread slices, toasted
      Grated Parmesan cheese

In blazer pan of chafing dish cook onion in butter over direct heat till lightly browned. Add broth, 1 1/3 cups water, and wine; heat. Ladle into soup bowls. Sprinkle toast slices with cheese; float on soup. Pass additional cheese, if desired. Makes 8 to 10 servings.

ASPARAGUS-CHEESE SOUP

  1 10-ounce package frozen cut
      asparagus
  1 tablespoon butter or margarine
  2 teaspoons all-purpose flour
  2 cups milk, scalded
  2 or 3 drops bottled hot pepper
      sauce (optional)
  4 ounces process American cheese,
      shredded (1 cup)

Cook asparagus according to package directions; drain. In blazer pan of chafing dish melt butter over direct heat; blend in flour. Add milk all at once; cook, stirring constantly, till thickened and bubbly. Add asparagus, 1/4 teaspoon salt, hot pepper sauce, and dash pepper; mix well. Add cheese; heat, stirring constantly, till melted. Makes 4 to 6 servings.

CREAM OF CORN SOUP

  1/4 cup finely chopped onion
  1/4 cup grated carrot
  2 tablespoons finely chopped
      green pepper
  2 tablespoons butter or margarine
  2 tablespoons all-purpose flour
  2 chicken bouillon cubes, crushed
  2 cups milk, scalded
  1 17-ounce can cream-style corn

In blazer pan of chafing dish cook onion, carrot, and green pepper with butter over direct heat till tender. Blend in flour and dash pepper. Add crushed bouillon, milk, and corn. Cook, stirring occasionally, till mixture bubbles. Makes 6 to 8 servings.

CIDER SNAP

  1 quart apple cider *or* apple juice
  2 tablespoons red cinnamon candies

Combine cider and cinnamon candies in blazer pan of chafing dish. Heat and stir over direct heat till candies are dissolved and cider is hot. Pour into mugs. Garnish each serving with an unpeeled apple slice and cinnamon stick, if desired. Makes 6 to 8 servings.

HOT TOMATO COCKTAIL

  1 46-ounce can tomato juice
      (about 6 cups)
  1 101/2-ounce can condensed beef
      broth
  1 teaspoon grated onion
  1 teaspoon prepared horseradish
  1 teaspoon Worcestershire sauce
  1 or 2 drops bottled hot pepper
      sauce
          . . .
  8 lemon twists
  8 cocktail onions

In blazer pan of chafing dish combine tomato juice, beef broth, onion, horseradish, Worcestershire sauce, and hot pepper sauce. Heat just to boiling. Ladle into cups. Garnish each serving with a twist of lemon and cocktail onion speared on a cocktail pick. Makes 8 servings.

SEAFOOD IN WINE

> 1 pound assorted frozen seafood (lobster, crab, shrimp, or scallops)
> ½ cup dry white wine
> ¼ cup salad oil
> 2 teaspoons minced onion
> 1 teaspoon sugar
> Dash dried rosemary leaves, crushed
> 2 tablespoons butter or margarine, melted
> 1 tablespoon lemon juice

Cook seafood following package directions; cool. (Remove meat from shells, if necessary.) Cut into bite-size pieces. Combine wine, oil, onion, sugar, ¼ teaspoon salt, rosemary, and dash pepper; pour over seafood. Marinate a few hours in refrigerator, stirring occasionally.

At serving time drain seafood, reserving marinade. Place seafood in blazer pan of chafing dish. Combine marinade, butter, and lemon juice. Pour over seafood. Heat gently over direct heat; keep warm over hot water. Spear with cocktail picks. Makes 50 appetizers.

MAPLED APPETIZERS

> 1 13½-ounce can pineapple chunks
> 2 8-ounce packages brown-and-serve sausage links
> 4 teaspoons cornstarch
> ½ teaspoon salt
> ½ cup maple-flavored syrup
> ⅓ cup water
> ⅓ cup vinegar
> 1 medium green pepper, cut in ¾-inch squares
> ½ cup drained maraschino cherries

Drain pineapple, reserving ½ cup syrup. Cut sausages in thirds crosswise; brown in skillet. At serving time blend cornstarch, salt, reserved syrup, maple-flavored syrup, water, and vinegar in blazer pan of chafing dish. Heat to boiling over direct heat, stirring constantly; cook and stir a few minutes more.

Add drained pineapple, sausage, green pepper chunks, and cherries; heat through. Keep warm over hot water (bain-marie). Spear with cocktail picks. Makes about 150 appetizers.

CRAB-STUFFED MUSHROOMS

> 1 pound fresh mushrooms, 1 to 1½ inches in diameter
> ¼ cup butter or margarine, melted
> 3 tablespoons fine dry bread crumbs
> 3 tablespoons butter or margarine, melted
> 2 tablespoons finely chopped celery
> 1 tablespoon finely chopped canned pimiento
> ½ teaspoon instant minced onion
> ¼ teaspoon dry mustard
> 1 7½-ounce can crab meat, drained, flaked, and cartilage removed
> • • •
> ½ cup dairy sour cream
> ½ cup mayonnaise or salad dressing
> 3 tablespoons milk
> 2 teaspoons lemon juice
> 1 teaspoon prepared mustard

Remove stems from mushrooms. Place unfilled mushrooms, rounded side up, on baking sheet. Brush tops with the ¼ cup melted butter. Broil 3 to 4 inches from heat for 2 to 3 minutes, till lightly browned. Remove from broiler.

Combine bread crumbs, the 3 tablespoons melted butter, celery, pimiento, onion, and dry mustard. Stir in crab meat. Turn mushrooms; fill each with crab mixture.

In flat blazer pan of chafing dish combine sour cream, mayonnaise, milk, lemon juice, and prepared mustard. Cook and stir over hot water (bain-marie) till hot. Arrange filled mushrooms, rounded side down, in sauce. Heat through. Makes 36 to 48 appetizers.

SAUCY SAUSAGES

> 2 8-ounce packages brown-and-serve sausage links
> 1 envelope spaghetti sauce mix
> 1¼ cups water

Cut sausages in thirds crosswise. Using canned tomato sauce variation, prepare spaghetti sauce mix following package directions *substituting* 1¼ cups water for the recommended amount. Pour into blazer pan of chafing dish. Add sausage; heat through over direct heat. Keep warm over hot water (bain-marie). Spear with cocktail picks. Makes about 65 appetizers.

SELF-SERVICE SUPPER

Summertime entertaining is effortless and spectacular when fast foods that boast gourmet flavors are served buffet-style.

MENU

Sweet-Sour Surprises
Herbed Chicken Salad
Whole Wheat Rolls   *Butter*
Fresh Pineapple in Shell
Punch

The menu initiates an evening of full-scale excitement, while the easy recipes take advantage of every precious minute you're in the

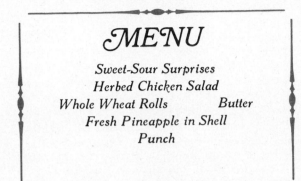

Glossy-sauced Sweet-Sour Surprises make an instant hit when appetites are waning. The chafing dish preserves the succulent pieces of shrimp, meatballs, and chicken livers at eating temperature.

kitchen. Note that Sweet-Sour Surprises heat together while you toss-up the main dish, heat the packaged rolls, and remove pre-prepared punch and pineapple from the refrigerator.

As hostess and guests eat at leisure, keep foods hot or cold in attractive servers—a stunning chafing dish keeps appetizers hot, beds of crushed ice hold chilly salad and refreshing fresh pineapple dessert, and piping hot rolls nestle in a bun warmer.

SWEET-SOUR SURPRISES

- 2 tablespoons cornstarch
- 2 tablespoons sugar
- 1 chicken bouillon cube
- 1 cup pineapple juice
- ⅓ cup vinegar
- 2 tablespoons soy sauce
- 1 tablespoon butter or margarine
- ½ pound tiny meatballs, cooked
- ½ pound shrimp, cooked, peeled, and cleaned
- ½ pound chicken livers, cooked and halved

In blazer pan of chafing dish combine first 3 ingredients. Add pineapple juice, ½ cup water, vinegar, soy, and butter. Cook and stir over direct heat till boiling. Cover; simmer 5 minutes. Arrange meats in sauce. Heat through. Keep warm over hot water (bain-marie). Spear with cocktail picks. Makes 60 to 65 appetizers.

HERBED CHICKEN SALAD

- 2 small heads romaine, torn in bite-size pieces (8 cups)
- 4 cups cubed cooked chicken, chilled
- ¼ cup grated Parmesan cheese
- 1 cup salad oil
- 6 tablespoons tarragon vinegar
- 1 teaspoon dry mustard
- 8 drops Worcestershire sauce
- 4 cups herb-seasoned stuffing croutons

Combine first 3 ingredients. Mix together next 4 ingredients and dash pepper. Pour *half* the dressing over croutons and toss (do not let croutons get soaked). Add croutons to salad with remaining dressing. Makes 16 servings.

MAIN DISHES – SIMPLE AND GOURMET

ELEGANT SALMON BALLS

1 16-ounce can salmon
1 cup soft bread crumbs (1½ slices)
2 eggs
2 tablespoons snipped parsley
1 tablespoon grated onion
2 teaspoons lemon juice
½ cup sauterne
2 tablespoons butter or margarine
3 tablespoons all-purpose flour
½ cup light cream
1 tablespoon snipped parsley
1 tablespoon drained capers

Drain salmon, reserving liquid. Remove salmon skin and bones; flake meat into bowl. Add bread crumbs, eggs, the 2 tablespoons parsley, onion, lemon juice, ½ teaspoon salt, and dash pepper; mix well. Shape into 8 balls.

Combine sauterne and reserved salmon liquid; add water to make 2 cups liquid. In skillet heat to boiling. Add salmon balls; return to boiling. Reduce heat; cover and simmer 10 minutes. Remove salmon balls; strain liquid.

In blazer pan of chafing dish melt butter over direct heat; blend in flour. Stir in the hot strained liquid. Cook and stir till thickened and bubbly. Stir in cream, the 1 tablespoon parsley, and capers. Place salmon balls in sauce; heat through. Makes 4 servings.

CLAM CHOWDER AU VIN

In saucepan combine 2 cups diced potato, 1 cup water, ½ cup chopped onion, ½ cup chopped celery, and ¼ teaspoon salt. Cook, covered, 10 minutes or till potatoes are tender; mash slightly. Whip ½ cup whipping cream; refrigerate.

In blazer pan of chafing dish combine mashed vegetables; one 10¾-ounce can condensed Manhattan-style clam chowder; 1 cup milk; one 7½-ounce can minced clams, drained; and 3 tablespoons dry white wine. Heat over direct heat but do not boil. Stir in whipped cream. Season with salt and pepper; sprinkle with 2 tablespoons snipped parsley. Serves 4.

SHRIMP NEWBURG

Bake 8 frozen patty shells according to package directions. In blazer pan of chafing dish combine two 10½-ounce cans condensed cream of shrimp soup and ½ cup milk; heat over direct heat. Add 2 cups cleaned, peeled, cooked shrimp and ½ of a 10-ounce package frozen peas. Continue to heat, stirring constantly, till just simmering. Cook slowly about 5 to 10 minutes.

Stir in ¼ cup dry sherry and ½ cup shredded sharp *natural* Cheddar cheese. Sprinkle an additional ½ cup Cheddar cheese in patty shells. Spoon newburg into shells. Serves 8.

LOBSTER NEWBURG

6 tablespoons butter or margarine
2 tablespoons all-purpose flour
1½ cups light cream
3 beaten egg yolks
1 5-ounce can lobster, drained, broken in large pieces, and cartilage removed
3 tablespoons dry white wine
2 teaspoons lemon juice
¼ teaspoon salt
Paprika
Toast Cups (see page 55)

In blazer pan of chafing dish melt butter over direct heat; blend in flour. Add cream all at once. Cook, stirring constantly, till thickened and bubbly. Place over hot water bath.

Stir small amount of hot mixture into beaten egg yolks; return to hot mixture. Cook, stirring constantly, till thickened. Add lobster; heat through. Stir in wine, lemon juice, and salt. Sprinkle with paprika. Serve in Toast Cups. Makes 4 or 5 servings.

Bright green peas and cooked shrimp swim in a → lightly-sherried cheese sauce in this exquisite version of classic Shrimp Newburg. Serve over shredded cheese inside the patty shells.

To prepare Classic Beef Stroganoff in a chafing dish, cook meat in blazer pan.

Remove meat to warm platter. Cook sauce in same pan stirring till thickened and bubbly.

Return meat to the blazer pan. Stir in sour cream and wine. Keep warm over bain-marie.

CLASSIC BEEF STROGANOFF

1 tablespoon all-purpose flour
1 pound beef sirloin, cut in
    1/4-inch strips
2 tablespoons butter or margarine
1 3-ounce can sliced mushrooms,
    drained
1/2 cup chopped onion
1 clove garlic, minced
2 tablespoons butter or margarine
3 tablespoons all-purpose flour
1 tablespoon tomato paste
1 1/4 cups beef stock *or* 1 10 1/2-ounce
    can condensed beef broth
1 cup dairy sour cream
2 tablespoons dry sherry
    Hot buttered noodles

Combine the 1 tablespoon flour and 1/2 teaspoon salt; coat meat with flour mixture. In blazer pan of chafing dish melt the first 2 tablespoons butter over direct heat; add meat and brown quickly on both sides. Add mushrooms, onion, and garlic; cook 3 or 4 minutes till onion is crisp-tender. Remove meat and mushrooms from pan.

Add remaining butter to pan drippings; blend in remaining flour. Add tomato paste; stir in cool meat stock. Cook and stir till thickened and bubbly. Return meat and mushrooms to blazer pan. Stir in sour cream and wine; cook slowly till heated through (do not boil). Keep warm over hot water (bain-marie). Serve over hot buttered noodles. Makes 4 servings.

BEER BEEF STROGANOFF

In blazer pan of chafing dish quickly brown 2 pounds beef sirloin, cut in 1/4-inch strips, in 2 tablespoons salad oil. Season with 1 1/2 teaspoons salt and 1/8 teaspoon pepper. Remove meat from pan. In same pan cook, covered, 2 medium onions, sliced, and one 3-ounce can undrained mushrooms for 3 to 4 minutes till onion is crisp-tender. Push to one side.

Blend 2 tablespoons all-purpose flour and 1/4 teaspoon paprika into pan drippings. Add 1 1/2 cups beer and 1 teaspoon Worcestershire sauce; cook and stir till thickened and bubbly. Return meat to pan. Stir in 1 cup dairy sour cream; cook slowly till heated through (do not boil). Keep warm over hot water (bain-marie). Serve over hot buttered noodles. Serves 6 to 8.

BURGUNDIED TENDERLOIN

1½ pounds beef tenderloin, cut in
    very thin 2- to 3-inch strips
6 tablespoons butter or margarine
2 medium green peppers, chopped
2 medium onions, chopped
1 10½-ounce can condensed beef
    broth
½ cup red Burgundy
1½ tablespoons cornstarch
    Hot cooked rice

Sprinkle meat with ½ teaspoon salt. Over direct heat melt *2 tablespoons* butter in blazer pan
of chafing dish. Brown a *third* of meat in butter;
remove to warm platter. Repeat twice with remaining meat adding butter as needed.

Add any remaining butter, green pepper, and
onion to pan; cook about 3 minutes. Add broth.
Combine wine and cornstarch; stir into vegetables. Cook, stirring constantly, till thickened
and bubbly. Cook and stir 2 minutes more. Season with salt and pepper. Add meat; heat
through. Serve over rice. Serves 6.

VEAL BERTRAND

2 pounds veal round steak *or*
    cutlets
1 6-ounce can whole mushrooms,
    drained
⅔ cup dry sherry
¼ cup snipped parsley
    Dash garlic powder
6 tablespoons butter or margarine
3 slices process Swiss cheese

Cut veal in 6 portions; pound to ¼-inch thickness. Slash edges with knife to prevent curling.
Combine mushrooms, sherry, parsley, and garlic. Pour mixture over meat. Marinate for 30
minutes, turning several times.

Over direct heat melt butter in blazer pan of
chafing dish. Drain meat, reserving marinade.
Quickly brown *half* the meat in butter, about 3
minutes on each side. Remove to warm serving
platter. Cook remaining meat.

Return meat to pan; add marinade and bring
to boiling. Reduce heat. Place cheese atop meat.
Cover; cook slowly about 2 minutes till cheese
melts. Transfer meat to warm serving platter.
Spoon hot sauce over. Makes 6 servings.

WESTERN WELSH RAREBIT

2 tablespoons butter or margarine
1 3-ounce can chopped mushrooms,
    drained
¼ cup finely chopped celery
2 tablespoons finely chopped green
    pepper
¼ cup all-purpose flour
2 teaspoons prepared mustard
1 teaspoon Worcestershire sauce
1 cup beer
1 pound process American cheese,
    shredded (4 cups)
    Toast Cups (see page 55)

In blazer pan melt butter over direct heat. Add
next 3 ingredients and cook till tender; remove
from heat. Blend in flour, mustard, and Worcestershire. Add beer all at once. Cook and stir till
thickened. Gradually add cheese; cook and stir
till cheese melts. If necessary, thin with a little
beer. Keep mixture warm over hot water. Serve
in Toast Cups. Makes 4 servings.

Keep natural cheese smooth in sauces by plac-
ing the sauce over hot water (bain-marie) before
adding the cheese. Add the crumbled, cubed, or
shredded cheese to the hot mixture and stir till melted.

HAM-APRICOT CREPES

1 cup sifted all-purpose flour
1 cup milk
1 slightly beaten egg
1 tablespoon butter or margarine, melted
10 thin slices boiled ham
1 8-ounce can apricot halves
2/3 cup sugar
2 tablespoons cornstarch
1 12-ounce can apricot nectar (1½ cups)
2 teaspoons lemon juice
2 tablespoons butter or margarine
¼ cup brandy (optional)

Combine flour, milk, egg, and the melted butter or margarine; beat till smooth. Lightly grease a 6-inch skillet; heat. Remove from heat and pour 2 tablespoons batter into skillet; quickly tilt pan from side to side till batter covers bottom. Return to heat; brown crepe on one side only. Repeat with remaining batter to make a total of 10 crepes.

To prepare sauce drain apricots, reserving syrup. Mix sugar, cornstarch, and dash salt in saucepan. Blend in reserved syrup. Add nectar. Cook and stir till slightly thickened and clear. Remove from heat; add lemon juice. Stir in the 2 tablespoons butter till melted.

Place a ham slice on unbrowned side of each crepe; roll up with ham on inside. Place crepes and apricot halves in blazer pan of chafing dish. Pour sauce over; cover and heat through over direct heat. In small saucepan heat brandy. Remove chafing dish cover; ignite brandy and spoon over crepes. Makes 5 servings.

NOODLE-BACON SCRAMBLE

Cook 2 ounces (1 cup) noodles according to package directions; drain. Crisp-cook and crumble 3 slices bacon. Beat 4 eggs, 3 tablespoons milk, ½ teaspoon salt, and dash pepper till blended. Stir in noodles and bacon.

In blazer pan of chafing dish melt 2 tablespoons butter or margarine over direct heat. Add egg-noodle mixture. Gently stir and fold, working from center to outside. Continue cooking and folding till eggs are fully cooked but still moist and glossy. Remove from heat; serve immediately. Makes 3 or 4 servings.

Entice brunch guests with Ham-Apricot Crepes. The crepes can be prepared ahead, then rolled up and heated in the sauce at serving time. For added glamour, spoon flaming brandy over crepes at the table.

CREAMY HAM TOWERS

An elegant luncheon main dish—

6 frozen patty shells, baked

• • •

1 11¼-ounce can condensed green pea soup
½ cup water
2 cups cubed fully-cooked ham
1/3 cup sliced pitted ripe olives
2 tablespoons snipped parsley
2 tablespoons chopped canned pimiento
½ cup dairy sour cream

Warm the baked patty shells at 325° for 5 minutes. Meanwhile, in blazer pan of chafing dish blend together soup and water; heat and stir over direct heat till boiling. Stir in cubed ham, sliced olives, snipped parsley, and chopped pimiento; heat through. Stir in sour cream; heat through (do not boil). Spoon into warm patty shells. Makes 6 servings.

CHICKEN FANTASIA

As shown opposite the contents page—

> 6 small chicken breasts (about
>   2½ pounds), boned and skinned
> 6 thin slices boiled ham
> 2 tablespoons butter or margarine
> ⅔ cup water
> ½ cup apricot preserves
> 2 tablespoons vinegar
> ½ teaspoon salt
> ½ teaspoon dry mustard
> 1 8¾-ounce can pineapple tidbits
> 2 tablespoons cornstarch
> ¼ cup brandy

Place chicken breasts, boned side up, on cutting board. Working from center out, pound chicken lightly to make cutlets about ¼ inch thick. Place a ham slice on each cutlet; tuck in sides and roll up jelly-roll fashion. Skewer or tie. In large skillet slowly brown chicken in butter. Stir in water, preserves, vinegar, salt, and dry mustard. Cook, covered, for 20 minutes.

Drain pineapple, reserving syrup. Blend cornstarch and reserved syrup. Stir cornstarch mixture and pineapple tidbits into sauce in skillet. Cook, uncovered, 15 minutes or till chicken is tender, turning chicken rolls once.

At serving time transfer chicken to blazer pan of chafing dish; garnish with canned apricot halves, if desired. Place over chafing dish burner. Pour sauce into heat-proof dish. In small saucepan warm brandy; at table pour brandy over sauce. Ignite immediately; spoon flaming sauce over chicken. Makes 6 servings.

CHICKEN ALOHA

In blazer pan of chafing dish cook 1 cup chopped celery and 1 green pepper, cut in thin strips (¾ cup), in 2 tablespoons salad oil over direct heat till crisp-tender. Stir in one 10½-ounce can condensed cream of chicken soup, *half* of a 22-ounce can pineapple pie filling*, ¼ cup water, and 2 tablespoons soy sauce. Add 2 cups cubed cooked chicken.

Cook, stirring occasionally, till hot. Serve over hot cooked rice. Garnish with ¼ cup toasted slivered almonds. Makes 6 servings.

*Use remaining pie filling later as topper for cake or ice cream.

DEUTSCH DINNER

As shown opposite section introduction—

> 5 slices bacon
> ½ cup chopped onion
> 1 cup mayonnaise or salad dressing
> 1 teaspoon celery seed
> 2 to 3 tablespoons vinegar
> 6 cups peeled, cubed, cooked
>   potatoes
> ½ pound skinless fully-cooked
>   knackwurst, cut in ½-inch slices
> ⅓ cup chopped sweet pickle
> 1 tablespoon chopped canned
>   pimiento
> 1 hard-cooked egg, sliced

In skillet cook bacon till crisp; drain and crumble, reserving ¼ cup fat. In blazer pan of chafing dish cook onion in reserved fat over direct heat till tender. Blend in mayonnaise, 1 teaspoon salt, celery seed, and dash pepper. Add ½ cup water and vinegar; cook and stir till bubbly. Add next 4 ingredients and bacon. Heat through, tossing lightly. Garnish with egg and parsley, if desired. Serves 5 or 6.

COTTAGE ENCHILADAS

Cook 9 frozen tortillas in water according to package directions. Combine one 12-ounce carton cream-style cottage cheese (1½ cups), 1 cup dairy sour cream, ½ teaspoon salt, and dash pepper. Reserve ½ *cup* of filling mixture; spoon 2 to 3 tablespoons remaining filling on each tortilla. Drain one 4-ounce can green chilies; cut chilies in 9 strips. Top filling of each tortilla with a strip of green chili; roll up.

In blazer pan of chafing dish combine reserved filling mixture; one 14-ounce can enchilada sauce; and 8 ounces sharp process American cheese, shredded (2 cups). Cook and stir over direct heat till cheese is melted. Add tortillas; heat through. Makes 4 or 5 servings.

TOAST CUPS

Trim crusts from 4 slices white bread; spread with ¼ cup softened butter. Carefully press into ungreased medium muffin cups. Toast at 350° for about 15 minutes. Makes 4 toast cups.

DINNER BY CANDLELIGHT

Gala centerpiece candles in distinctive colors, shapes, and textures transform ordinary menus into elegant dinners. They help to make dinner a romantic occasion.

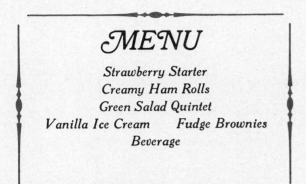

MENU

Strawberry Starter
Creamy Ham Rolls
Green Salad Quintet
Vanilla Ice Cream   Fudge Brownies
Beverage

Candlelight dining creates a relaxed, enjoyable mood. Low lights and soft music add charm. A formal atmosphere suggests linen tablecloth, fresh-flower-and-candle centerpiece, fine china and glassware, and sterling silver.

Prefer the more casual? Show off the rich wood-grain tabletop and protect place settings with colored straw mats. For eating and serving equipment, choose pottery, glass goblets, and stainless steel. A centerpiece grouping of stout candles reflects informality.

This menu combines elegance with simplicity —frequently it's the easily-made foods that are most well-received. Hours before dinner, take a few minutes to prepare a yogurt dressing and to spoon strawberries into serving dishes—then refrigerate. The rice-filled ham and the onion sauce are also prepared ahead. Heated together at the table in a chafing dish, they become Creamy Ham Rolls.

Combine salad vegetables, cover with moist paper toweling, and refrigerate. Dressing is tossed in before dinner begins. Brownies made the day before from scratch or mix, and served with ice cream are a delicious meal ending.

← **Accented by candlelight,** Creamy Ham Rolls provide an attractive entree prepared with convenience foods. Packaged rice with peas, mushrooms, and cheese peek from ham rolls nestled in saucy onions.

STRAWBERRY STARTER

Rinse, hull, and halve fresh strawberries (or use frozen unsweetened strawberries, partially thawed). Spoon into sherbet dishes. Combine one 8-ounce carton strawberry-flavored yogurt, ¼ cup sugar, and few drops red food coloring. Drizzle over berries. Garnish with mint sprigs.

GREEN SALAD QUINTET

  ½ bunch watercress
  6 romaine leaves
  6 Boston lettuce leaves
  4 escarole leaves
  2 Belgian endives
  6 radishes, sliced
  1 scallion, finely chopped
    • • •
  2 tablespoons olive *or* salad oil
  2 tablespoons wine vinegar
    Dash *each* garlic salt, paprika, and freshly ground pepper

Rinse first 5 ingredients; drain. Tear leaves in bite-size pieces and slice endives. Combine greens with radishes and scallion. Combine remaining ingredients. Toss lightly with lettuce mixture. Makes 4 to 6 servings.

CREAMY HAM ROLLS

  1 12-ounce package frozen rice with peas and mushrooms
  2 ounces sharp process American cheese, shredded (½ cup)
  8 slices boiled ham
  1 10-ounce package frozen onions in cream sauce
  1 envelope white sauce mix

Prepare frozen rice according to package directions. (Omit Parmesan cheese if called for.) Stir in American cheese; spoon about ¼ *cup* on each ham slice. Roll up jelly-roll fashion. Prepare frozen onions in cream sauce according to package directions.

In blazer pan of large chafing dish prepare white sauce mix over direct heat following package directions. Add cooked onions with cream sauce; arrange ham rolls in sauce. Cover and heat through. Makes 4 servings.

SHOW-STOPPING DINNER

A host-and-hostess team act out this impressive cooked-at-the-table dinner. First, the host tosses together Original Caesar Salad; then the hostess cooks Steak Diane.

MENU

Original Caesar Salad
Steak Diane
Twice-Baked Potatoes
Hot Rolls   Jam and Jelly
Cheesecake
Beverage

Their cooking performance will appear well-rehearsed as a result of skillful planning and behind-the-scenes organization. The co-hosts, like actors, should know their recipes thoroughly, thinking through and becoming familiar with each step of preparation.

To help the recipes go together smoothly, they should prepare ahead any foods that require kitchen equipment. Potatoes are baked and stuffed early in the day. For Original Caesar Salad, romaine is torn into a large salad bowl and chilled. Oil, vinegar, lemon, egg, cheese, and croutons are measured into individual dishes. The entree steaks are seasoned and pounded, garnish mushrooms fluted, and lemon juice, Worcestershire sauce, chives, and butter measured separately.

The table is set with one "stage" at each end. Carefully arranged trays at each cooking center contain all the necessary ingredients and cooking tools. The salad chef needs torn romaine and premeasured salad ingredients as well as Worcestershire sauce, salt and pepper shakers, salad tossing and serving pieces, and individual salad bowls. In addition to the ingredients for Steak Diane, the hostess must have chafing dish, cooking tongs, and spoon.

Meanwhile, in the oven twice-baked potatoes and convenience rolls heat shortly before guests are seated. Both foods stay hot on a convenient warming tray until salad and main dish are artfully prepared and served.

ORIGINAL CAESAR SALAD

Break 2 small heads romaine, chilled, in 2- or 3-inch widths into salad bowl. Drizzle with about 3 tablespoons Garlic Olive Oil, then 1 to 1½ tablespoons wine vinegar. Squeeze ½ lemon over; break in one 1-minute coddled egg.

Season with salt and dash Worcestershire sauce. Grind pepper over all. Sprinkle with 3 tablespoons grated Parmesan cheese. Roll-toss 6 or 7 times, or till dressing is well combined and every leaf is coated. Add about ½ cup Caesar Croutons; toss once or twice. Serve at once. Garnish with rolled anchovy fillets, if desired. Makes 5 or 6 servings.

Garlic Olive Oil: Prepare mixture one to several days ahead. Slice 3 cloves garlic in quarters; let stand in ½ cup olive oil (*or* salad oil *or* half olive oil and half salad oil).

Caesar Croutons: Cut bread slice into ¾-inch cubes. Spread out on baking sheet; pour a little Garlic Olive Oil over. Heat at 225° for 2 hours. Sprinkle with grated Parmesan cheese. Store, covered, in jar in refrigerator.

STEAK DIANE

    4 top loin (strip) beef steaks,
        cut ½ inch thick
    1 teaspoon dry mustard
    ¼ cup butter or margarine
    3 tablespoons lemon juice
    2 teaspoons snipped chives
    1 teaspoon Worcestershire sauce

With meat mallet pound steaks to ⅓-inch thickness. Sprinkle *each side* with salt, freshly ground pepper, and ⅛ *teaspoon* of the dry mustard; pound into meat.

In blazer pan of chafing dish melt butter over direct heat. Add 2 steaks; cook 2 minutes on each side. Transfer to hot serving plate. Repeat for remaining meat. To blazer pan add remaining ingredients; bring to boiling. Return meat to pan; spoon sauce over. Trim with cooked, fluted mushrooms, if desired. Makes 4 servings.

Guests watch in amazement as exquisite Steak →
Diane is artistically cooked before their eyes. This West Coast-inspired recipe dresses up tender and juicy top loin steaks by means of distinctive seasoning.

DESSERTS TO DAZZLE

GRAPE-SYRUPED CREPES

    1 cup sifted all-purpose flour
    1 tablespoon sugar
1½ cups milk
    2 eggs
1½ teaspoons grated lemon peel
    2 teaspoons lemon juice
  ½ teaspoon vanilla
    1 4-ounce container whipped
       cream cheese
  ⅓ cup chopped pecans
    1 6-ounce can frozen grape juice
       concentrate, thawed (⅔ cup)
    4 teaspoons cornstarch
    2 tablespoons sugar

In mixing bowl combine flour, sugar, milk, eggs, ½ *teaspoon* lemon peel, lemon juice, and vanilla; beat till smooth. Lightly grease a 6-inch skillet; heat. Remove from heat; spoon in about 2 tablespoons batter. Rotate pan so batter is spread evenly over bottom. Return to heat; brown on one side only. To remove, invert pan over paper toweling.

Repeat with remaining batter, greasing pan occasionally. Spread unbrowned side of each crepe with cream cheese and sprinkle with pecans. Roll up.

In blazer pan of chafing dish gradually stir grape juice into cornstarch. Add ½ cup water. Cook quickly over direct heat, stirring constantly, till thickened and bubbly. Stir in sugar and the remaining lemon peel. Add filled crepes. Heat through. Garnish with additional shredded lemon peel, if desired. Serves 6.

GOLDEN RAISIN FLAMBE

In saucepan cover ½ cup light raisins with water. Bring to boil; simmer 5 minutes. Drain. Add ¼ cup brandy, 3 tablespoons brown sugar, ¼ teaspoon grated lemon peel, and 1 tablespoon lemon juice. Cover; let stand 1 hour.

At serving time transfer raisin mixture to blazer pan of small chafing dish. Bring to boil over direct heat. In small saucepan heat ¼ cup brandy. Ignite; spoon over sauce. Serve sauce over vanilla ice cream. Serves 6.

CREPES SUZETTE

  ⅔ cup sifted all-purpose flour
    2 tablespoons sugar
1½ cups milk
    2 eggs
    2 egg yolks
    2 tablespoons butter or margarine,
       melted
       • • •
  ½ cup butter or margarine
  ½ cup sugar
    2 teaspoons grated orange peel
    1 teaspoon grated lemon peel
  ¼ cup orange juice
    1 tablespoon lemon juice
       Confectioners' sugar
  ¼ cup orange-flavored liqueur

In mixing bowl combine first six ingredients and ⅛ teaspoon salt. Beat till smooth. Lightly grease a 6-inch skillet; heat. Remove from heat; spoon in about 2 tablespoons batter. Rotate pan so batter is spread evenly over bottom. Return to heat; brown on one side only. To remove, invert pan over paper toweling. Repeat with remaining batter, greasing pan occasionally. Keep warm till served.

Cream the ½ cup butter and ½ cup sugar; add grated peels and fruit juices. Spread about 1 tablespoon cream filling on each crepe. Roll up; sprinkle with confectioners' sugar.

At serving time arrange filled crepes in blazer pan of chafing dish; place over chafing dish burner. In small saucepan heat liqueur. Ignite; spoon over crepes. Makes 6 servings.

PEACH SAUCE

Drain one 29-ounce can peach slices, reserving syrup. In blazer pan of chafing dish gradually blend reserved syrup into 1 tablespoon cornstarch. Add 2 tablespoons butter or margarine, 2 teaspoons lemon juice, ½ teaspoon grated orange peel, ¼ teaspoon ground nutmeg, and ⅛ teaspoon almond extract. Cook over direct heat, stirring constantly, till thickened and bubbly. Add peaches; heat through. Serve over cake or shortcake. Makes 8 servings.

MANDARIN PEARS

Drain one 29-ounce can pear halves and one 11-ounce can mandarin oranges, reserving *1 cup* combined syrups. In blazer pan of chafing dish blend 1 tablespoon cornstarch, dash ground cloves, and dash ground nutmeg. Gradually stir in reserved syrup. Add ½ cup orange marmalade, 1 tablespoon lemon juice, and 1 tablespoon butter. Cook over direct heat, stirring constantly, till thickened and bubbly.

Add pear halves, cavity side up. Place 3 or 4 mandarin orange sections in each pear cavity. Heat through, spooning sauce over all. In small saucepan heat ¼ cup orange-flavored liqueur, if desired. Ignite and spoon over pears before serving. Makes 7 or 8 servings.

SAUTEED BANANAS

Cut 2 large firm bananas in half both lengthwise and crosswise. Brush with lemon juice. Combine 1 well-beaten egg and 1 tablespoon water. Dip bananas in egg mixture, then in ¾ cup vanilla wafer *or* graham cracker crumbs. In blazer pan of chafing dish melt ¼ cup butter over direct heat. Add bananas; fry till browned. Serve hot with Custard Sauce. Serves 4.

Custard Sauce: In heavy saucepan mix 4 beaten egg yolks, ¼ cup sugar, and dash salt. Gradually stir in 2 cups milk. Cook over low heat, stirring constantly, till mixture coats a metal spoon. Remove from heat. Cool pan immediately in ice water; stir for a minute or two. Add 1 teaspoon vanilla. Chill.

Delicate cream cheese-and-nut-filled lemon crepes are liberally drizzled with a royal grape sauce in Grape-Syruped Crepes. Avoid last-minute rush by making the crepes beforehand. At serving time the filled crepes are quickly reheated in the sauce made in the blazer pan of a chafing dish.

CHEESE-FILLED PEARS

>   3 fresh pears, peeled, halved,
>   and cored*
>   1/3 cup sugar
>   2 tablespoons brandy
>   1/4 teaspoon grated lemon peel
>   1 tablespoon lemon juice
>   1 3-ounce package cream cheese,
>   softened
>   1 ounce blue cheese,
>   crumbled (1/4 cup)
>   1/4 cup finely chopped pecans
>   1/4 cup brandy

In saucepan cook pears, covered, with 1 cup water and sugar till tender, about 10 minutes. Transfer pears, cavity side up, and liquid to blazer pan of chafing dish. Add the 2 tablespoons brandy, lemon peel, and juice.

In small bowl blend together cheeses. Shape into 6 balls; roll in nuts. Place one ball in cavity of each pear. Heat through over direct heat. In small saucepan heat the 1/4 cup brandy. Ignite and spoon over pears. Makes 6 servings.

*One 29-ounce can pear halves may be substituted for the fresh fruit. Drain pears, reserving *1 cup* syrup. Place halves, cavity side up, in blazer pan. Add reserved syrup, brandy, lemon peel, and juice. Proceed as above.

HOT FRUIT MEDLEY

Wine and cinnamon add intrigue—

>   1 13 1/2-ounce can pineapple chunks
>   1 16-ounce can apricot halves
>   1 16-ounce can peach halves
>   1 16-ounce can pitted dark sweet
>   cherries
>   1/4 cup brown sugar
>   1/4 teaspoon ground cinnamon
>   1/3 cup port
>   1 tablespoon lemon juice

Drain pineapple and apricots, reserving *all* of pineapple syrup and 1/2 *cup* of apricot syrup. Drain other fruits well; set aside. In blazer pan of chafing dish, blend together sugar and cinnamon; add reserved syrups, port, and lemon juice. Heat over direct heat till bubbly. Add pineapple, apricots, and peaches; heat through. Add cherries. Makes 8 servings.

In the first cooking stage of Cafe Brulot, orange peel, lemon peel, and spices sizzle in flaming cognac. Make this steamy after-dinner drink, as made in New Orleans restaurants, your cook-at-the-table specialty.

BLUEBERRY DUMPLINGS

>   1 15-ounce can blueberries
>   1/3 cup sugar
>   2 teaspoons cornstarch
>   Dash salt
>   1 tablespoon lemon juice
>   1 package refrigerated biscuits
>   (6 biscuits)
>   1/4 cup sugar
>   1/4 teaspoon ground cinnamon

Drain blueberries, reserving syrup; add enough water to syrup to make 1 cup. In blazer pan of chafing dish mix together the 1/3 cup sugar, cornstarch, and salt; gradually stir in syrup. Cook and stir over direct heat till thickened and bubbly. Stir in blueberries and lemon juice; return to boiling.

Dip biscuits in water, then roll in mixture of the 1/4 cup sugar and cinnamon. Place biscuits in bubbly sauce (do not overlap); cover. Cook 8 to 10 minutes or till done. Serve with cream, if desired. Makes 6 servings.

PEACH BETTY

6 tablespoons butter or margarine
¼ cup brown sugar
½ teaspoon ground cinnamon
4 cups small dry bread cubes
1 21-ounce can peach pie filling
½ teaspoon grated lemon peel
1 tablespoon lemon juice
Ground nutmeg

In blazer pan of chafing dish melt butter over direct heat. Blend in sugar and cinnamon. Add dry bread cubes; cook, tossing constantly, till browned. Stir in pie filling, lemon peel, and juice. Cook 5 minutes more or till heated through, stirring occasionally. Sprinkle with nutmeg. Serve with cream, if desired. Serves 6.

CAFE BRULOT

12 sugar cubes
1 tablespoon orange peel cut in thin slivers
1 teaspoon lemon peel cut in thin slivers
4 inches stick cinnamon
6 whole cloves
⅔ cup cognac *or* brandy
4 cups strong hot coffee

In blazer pan of chafing dish combine sugar, orange peel, lemon peel, cinnamon, and cloves. Add *half* the brandy and heat over direct heat till bubbly; ignite. Combine remaining brandy and coffee. Stir into spice mixture. Ladle into demitasse cups. Makes 8 servings.

DAIQUIRI BLAZER

An exotic sipper for before or after dinner—

In blazer pan of chafing dish combine 1½ cups hot water, ¼ cup sugar, 6 inches stick cinnamon, and 8 whole cloves. Bring to boiling over direct heat; cook 5 minutes. Add one 6-ounce can frozen lemonade concentrate, thawed, and one 6-ounce can frozen limeade concentrate, thawed; return to boiling.

In small saucepan heat ⅔ cup light rum; ignite. Pour over hot beverage. Ladle into demitasse cups. Makes 8 to 10 servings.

BUTTERSCOTCH-NUT SAUCE

1 3¾-ounce package *regular* butterscotch pudding mix
⅓ cup dark corn syrup
⅓ cup chunk-style peanut butter
1¼ cups milk
8 slices sponge cake, angel cake, pound cake, *or* vanilla ice cream

In blazer pan of chafing dish combine pudding mix, corn syrup, and peanut butter; gradually stir in milk. Cook and stir over direct heat till thickened and bubbly. Cook 2 minutes more. Spoon over cake or ice cream. Serves 6.

MOCHA SAUCE

1 cup sugar
⅓ cup unsweetened cocoa powder
1 tablespoon cornstarch
1 tablespoon instant coffee powder
1 14½-ounce can evaporated milk
¼ teaspoon vanilla
Vanilla ice cream

In blazer pan of chafing dish combine first 4 ingredients. Gradually stir in milk. Cook over direct heat, stirring constantly, till thickened and bubbly. Remove from heat; stir in vanilla. Spoon over ice cream. Serves 6.

NUTMEG-PINEAPPLE SAUCE

½ cup granulated sugar
½ cup brown sugar
½ cup light corn syrup
¼ cup butter or margarine
½ teaspoon ground nutmeg
1 13½-ounce can pineapple tidbits, drained
¼ teaspoon vanilla
10 slices sponge cake, angel cake, pound cake, *or* vanilla ice cream

In blazer pan of chafing dish combine first 5 ingredients. Cook over direct heat, stirring constantly, till mixture boils. Stir in pineapple and vanilla. Spoon hot pineapple sauce over cake or ice cream. Makes 10 servings.

DINNER ON THE PATIO

Cherries Jubilee, often thought to be an elegant dessert served indoors, can also be an outdoor finale as this menu illustrates.

MENU

Wine-Broiled Chicken
Tangy Cauliflower Bowl
Buttered Peas
Brown-and-Serve Rolls   Butter
Cherries Jubilee
Beverage

Behind the scenes, less picturesque tasks are performed. Appoint the man of the house as family chef and have him barbecue the chicken while the hostess prepares the rest of the meal. Toss the Tangy Cauliflower Bowl in advance, then garnish just before serving. Add convenience foods like frozen buttered peas and brown-and-serve rolls and there's plenty of time to devote to the flaming dessert.

The secret to presenting Cherries Jubilee with a flourish is to have cooking and serving equipment arranged on a cart. Thicken the cherry sauce before dinner begins and keep warm in the chafing dish; measure brandy into a saucepan. Ice cream, prescooped into serving dishes and frozen, is set in a bowl of crushed ice.

As the main course draws to a close, patio lights are dimmed; the hostess wheels on the cart. In seconds, amidst oohs and ahs, she flames and serves festive Cherries Jubilee.

TANGY CAULIFLOWER BOWL

Separate 1 medium head cauliflower into buds; cut each in half lengthwise. Combine with 2 medium carrots, cut in julienne strips; toss with 1/3 cup French-style salad dressing. Cover; refrigerate, stirring once or twice.

At serving time sprinkle with 2 tablespoons crumbled blue cheese. Toss lightly; spoon into lettuce cups. Top each serving with slices from 1 small avocado, peeled. Serves 6.

WINE-BROILED CHICKEN

Basting sauce gives the chicken a golden glow—

- 1/4 cup sauterne
- 1/4 cup soy sauce
- 2 tablespoons salad oil
- 2 tablespoons finely chopped onion
- 1/2 teaspoon dry mustard
- 3 1½-pound ready-to-cook chickens, halved lengthwise

Combine sauterne, soy sauce, salad oil, onion, and mustard; mix well. Cover and let stand several hours at room temperature or overnight in refrigerator. Brush meat with wine mixture.

Place chicken, skin side down, on grill. Cook over medium coals 20 minutes or till lightly browned, brushing occasionally with wine mixture. Turn chicken halves; broil 15 to 20 minutes longer or till done, brushing occasionally with wine mixture. Makes 6 servings.

CHERRIES JUBILEE

- 1 16-ounce can pitted dark sweet cherries
- 1/4 cup sugar
- 2 tablespoons cornstarch
- 1/4 cup brandy, kirsch, *or* cherry brandy
  Vanilla ice cream

Drain cherries, reserving syrup. Add cold water to syrup to make 1 cup. In saucepan blend sugar and cornstarch; gradually stir in syrup-water mixture, mixing well. Cook and stir over medium heat till mixture is thickened and bubbly. Remove from heat; stir in cherries. Turn mixture into blazer pan of chafing dish. Set pan over hot water (bain-marie).

Heat brandy in small saucepan. (If desired, pour heated brandy into large ladle.) Ignite and pour over cherry mixture. Stir to blend brandy into sauce. Serve immediately over vanilla ice cream. Makes 6 to 8 servings.

Indoors or outdoors, create showmanship and →
style by flaming classic Cherries Jubilee. The luscious dark sweet cherries, couched in a brandy-flavored sauce, are ladled over mounds of vanilla ice cream.

TABLETOP CUISINE

The myriad of smartly-styled appliances for tabletop cooking gives the modern homemaker another approach to dining. Some provide sufficient heat to cook table-side; others simply keep foods at serving temperature.

Cook-at-the-table units may be designed to cook only one or many types of foods. The versatility of electric skillets and griddles is well-known, but less familiar portable ovens and burners are equally handy. Specialized units are geared to cook one food to perfection—one solely cooks eggs; others, broilable meats or popcorn.

On the other side of tabletop cuisine, special servers in many sizes and styles keep foods hot or cold without flavor or texture loss. One course or an entire meal can be maintained at a just-right flavor and temperature.

Portable appliances used for tabletop cooking are attuned to today's trend towards convenience. Properly treated, they give maximum service with minimum care (see page 92).

COOKING UNITS COME TO THE TABLE

There are many different forms of cooking units which can move to the table. Besides the now-popular fondue pots and chafing dishes, enterprising hosts and hostesses are using table-size burners that include hot plates and the Orient-inspired hibachi. Each type can be used to establish an entertaining theme.

Table burner designs include grillwork on which to set a cooking utensil with heating element beneath. Some are single burner units; others have double burners for simultaneous cooking. Burner fuels include electricity, gas, butane, alcohol, or canned heat (see pages 42-43). Everyday pots and pans or more decorative cooking equipment can be used to cook quick and showy recipes.

Hibachis, small and large, operate most efficiently in well-ventilated rooms, particularly on porches and patios. Conventional hibachi fireboxes are made of heavy-duty cast iron. Used like other barbecue grills, hibachis have grids (some adjustable) and draft doors.

TERIYAKI APPETIZERS

  1½ pounds top sirloin steak, cut
      1 inch thick
            • • •
  ½ cup soy sauce
  ¼ cup brown sugar
  2 tablespoons salad oil
  1 tablespoon grated fresh
      gingerroot *or* 1 teaspoon ground
      ginger
  ¼ teaspoon freshly ground pepper
  2 cloves garlic, minced
      Canned water chestnuts, halved

Partially freeze meat then slice in very thin strips. In deep bowl combine next 6 ingredients; mix well. Add meat and water chestnuts; toss gently to coat. Let stand 2 hours at room temperature. Drain meat, reserving marinade.

Thread meat strips on metal skewers accordion-style; than add a water chestnut. Broil over hot coals 5 to 6 minutes, turning frequently while basting with marinade. Serves 6 to 8.

LEMONY-SHRIMP KABOBS

Inviting for appetizers or main course—

  ½ cup chili sauce
  ¼ cup salad oil
  2 tablespoons dark corn syrup
  2 tablespoons vinegar
  ½ clove garlic
  ¼ teaspoon pepper
  2 pounds shrimp, peeled and cleaned
  1 or 2 lemons, cut in wedges

In blender container combine chili sauce, salad oil, corn syrup, vinegar, garlic, ½ teaspoon salt, and pepper; cover and blend on high speed of blender till sauce is smooth.

If desired, wrap tails of shrimp with aluminum foil to prevent burning during broiling. Thread lemon wedges and shrimp on skewers. Broil over medium coals of hibachi 6 to 8 minutes on each side, brushing with sauce occasionally. To serve, squeeze juice from hot lemon wedges over shrimp. Makes 10 to 12 appetizer servings or 6 main course servings.

BEEF AND FRUIT KABOBS

  ¾ pound round steak, cut in 1-inch
      cubes
      Instant meat tenderizer
  1 11-ounce can mandarin oranges
  1 13½-ounce can pineapple chunks,
      drained
  ½ cup brown sugar
  ¼ cup honey
  1 tablespoon butter or margarine,
      melted

Use meat tenderizer on beef following label directions. Drain oranges, reserving ¼ cup syrup. Alternate meat and fruit on four 6-inch skewers. (Skewer oranges crosswise.) Combine reserved syrup and remaining ingredients. Broil kabobs over hot coals of hibachi about 10 minutes, turn to brown on all sides and basting frequently with sauce. Serves 2.

Colorful pillows help create a realistic setting for this out-of-the-East dinner. The delectable main course, Beef and Fruit Kabobs, sports a subtle honey-fruit marinade. Here the kabobs cook on a hibachi placed table-side, but a smaller unit can be set directly on the dining table, if desired.

VEAL CORDON BLEU

Ham and cheese are sandwiched between the veal—

> 1 **pound veal round steak *or* cutlets, cut ¼ inch thick**
> 4 **thin slices boiled ham, cut in half**
> 4 **slices process Swiss cheese, cut in half**
>
> . . .
>
> ¼ **cup sifted all-purpose flour**
> 1 **slightly beaten egg**
> 1 **cup fine dry bread crumbs**
> ¼ **cup butter or margarine**
>
> . . .
>
> ¼ **cup dry white wine**

Cut veal round steak or cutlets into 8 pieces. With meat mallet pound each piece very thin to about ⅛-inch thickness.

If necessary, trim halved slices of ham and Swiss cheese so that they are slightly smaller than the veal pieces. Top a veal piece with 2 half-slices of ham and 2 half-slices of Swiss cheese. Place another veal piece over the meat stack. Press edges together to seal. Repeat with remaining veal, ham, and cheese.

Coat meat with flour. Dip in egg, then in bread crumbs. In large skillet melt butter over tabletop burner. Brown meat in butter over medium heat till golden brown, about 5 minutes on each side. Remove to warm platter. Swish out skillet with wine then spoon wine over meat. Makes 4 servings.

BEEF-CAULIFLOWER COMBO

    2 tablespoons dry sherry
    ⅛ teaspoon salt
      Dash pepper
    1 pound sirloin steak, very thinly
      sliced across the grain
    2 tablespoons salad oil
    2 tablespoons cornstarch
    1 10½-ounce can condensed beef
      broth
    2 tablespoons sugar
    2 tablespoons soy sauce
    1 tablespoon vinegar
    2 cups cooked cauliflowerets
    1 9-ounce package frozen Italian
      green beans, cooked and
      drained
      Hot cooked rice

In mixing bowl combine sherry, salt, and pepper. Add meat, mixing to coat well. Let stand 10 minutes at room temperature.

In skillet over tabletop burner brown meat mixture quickly in hot oil. Blend together cornstarch and beef broth; add to meat along with ¼ cup water, sugar, soy sauce, and vinegar.

Cook and stir till thickened and bubbly. Add cauliflower and beans; stir to coat. Heat through. Serve over rice. Makes 6 servings.

CANTONESE SHRIMP

    1 tablespoon salad oil
    1 7-ounce package frozen Chinese
      pea pods
    ¾ cup chicken broth
    1 5-ounce can water chestnuts,
      drained and sliced (⅔ cup)
    1 tablespoon cornstarch
    2 tablespoons cold water
    1 4½-ounce can shrimp, drained

Heat oil in skillet over tabletop burner. Add frozen pea pods; heat till thawed, separating with a fork. Stir in chicken broth, water chestnuts, and ¼ teaspoon salt. Cover and cook for 2 minutes, stirring once or twice.

Combine cornstarch and cold water; add to mixture in skillet. Cook, stirring constantly, till mixture is thickened and clear, about 2 minutes. Add drained shrimp; toss gently to mix. Heat through. Makes 2 or 3 servings.

FRENCH MUSHROOM OMELET

An elegant egg dish—

    3 eggs
    1 tablespoon water
    ¼ teaspoon salt
      Dash pepper
      Dash mixed herbs
    1 tablespoon butter or margarine
      Sauteed sliced fresh mushrooms*
      or one 3-ounce can sliced
      mushrooms, drained

In mixing bowl combine eggs, water, salt, pepper, and mixed herbs; beat just till mixture is blended but not frothy.

In 8-inch skillet with flared sides heat butter till it sizzles over tabletop burner. Tilt pan to grease sides. Pour in egg mixture, leaving heat moderately high. With fork, tines up, rapidly stir through top of uncooked egg, keeping omelet an even depth. Shake pan all the while to keep omelet sliding. Cook till set but still shiny, about 2 minutes.

Remove pan from heat; spoon mushrooms over *half* the omelet. With wide spatula lift and fold omelet over mushrooms. Slip out of skillet onto warm platter. Makes 1 or 2 servings.

*In skillet cook 1 cup sliced fresh mushrooms in 1 to 2 tablespoons butter till tender.

CHUCK WAGON MACARONI

A quick main dish for vacation days—

    1 7-ounce package macaroni
      (2 cups)
    ½ cup butter or margarine
    ¼ cup chili sauce
    1 teaspoon Worcestershire sauce
    8 ounces sharp process American
      cheese, shredded (2 cups)
      Paprika (optional)

In large saucepan cook macaroni according to package directions; drain well. Return cooked macaroni to saucepan and place over tabletop burner. Add butter, chili sauce, and Worcestershire sauce; heat and stir till butter is melted. Add cheese; stir till melted and well mixed. Sprinkle with paprika, if desired. Serve immediately. Makes 4 to 6 servings.

COOKING ON A HOT PLATE

A hot plate is convenient for cooking when a range is not available. Designed with one or two burners, they are easy to transport and can be moved to the site of the meal so long as an electrical outlet is handy.

MENU

Vegetable-Oyster Stew
Chef's Salad in a Roll
Sliced Peaches
Chocolate Haystacks
Milk

A quick dress-up for canned soup is Vegetable-Oyster Stew, prepared and kept warm over a portable hot plate. Man-sized Chef's Salad in a Roll completes the entree. For dessert, offer fruit with cookies.

Meals in which only one or two hot foods are served, such as breakfast or lunch, can be prepared on a hot plate. Lunch may include a hot soup accompanied with a salad or sandwich. Or, plan a skillet main dish and serve with a salad and fruit. Equipped with variable temperature settings, a hot plate can also double as a food warmer on the buffet table.

VEGETABLE-OYSTER STEW

In a saucepan over hot plate burner combine 1 cup shredded carrot, 2 tablespoons finely chopped onion, and ¼ cup water. Cook, covered, till carrot is tender, about 5 minutes.

Add two 10¼-ounce cans condensed oyster stew, 2 cups milk, and dash pepper. Heat just to boiling, stirring occasionally. Serves 4 or 5.

CHOCOLATE HAYSTACKS

In saucepan combine 2 cups sugar, ½ cup milk, ½ cup butter or margarine, and ⅓ cup unsweetened cocoa powder; bring to a full boil. Remove from heat. Stir in 3½ cups quick-cooking rolled oats, 1 cup flaked coconut, ½ cup chopped walnuts, ½ teaspoon vanilla, and dash salt. Drop quickly from teaspoon onto waxed paper; cool. Makes about 48 cookies.

CHEF'S SALAD IN A ROLL

Quick and easy to assemble—

> 4 **French rolls**
> **Butter or margarine, softened**
> **Romaine**
> 4 **ounces sharp process American cheese, cut in julienne strips**
> 4 **slices pressed ham**
> 4 **slices salami**
> 2 **hard-cooked eggs, sliced**
> **French-style salad dressing**

Split rolls lengthwise, *cutting to but not through* crust at back. Spread cut surfaces of rolls with softened butter or margarine.

For each sandwich: Cover bottom half of roll with romaine, then a few cheese strips, and a slice of pressed ham and salami, *each* folded in half. Place egg slices atop meat. Drizzle each sandwich with about 1 tablespoon French dressing. Anchor tops of rolls with wooden picks, if needed. Makes 4 servings.

ELECTRIC SKILLET TIME-SAVERS

Versatility is the key word for the electric skillet, one of the most popular portable cooking appliances sold. This compact unit is adaptable to all types of cook-at-the-table dinners.

Tiny appetizer meatballs in a spicy tomato sauce stay at eating temperature in the thermostatically-controlled skillet. If you are an Oriental food fan, this appliance is made to order for stir-fry dishes. For a meal-in-a-hurry, bring out the convenience foods, then whip up a main dish in the skillet. Serving pancakes for breakfast? The electric skillet can cook them to a delicate brownness. Desserts are served at the peak of perfection when cooked during the meal in the portable electric skillet.

Don't forget the teen-agers. They'll love the electric skillet for popping popcorn, frying onion rings, heating ground meat mixtures, and cooking hot dogs. When it's party time, this handy appliance keeps the food hot so the hungry young people can return for several helpings.

Want to color-key your appliances and kitchen? Electric skillets come in a rainbow of colors to fit your needs. These colorful skillets double as attractive serving dishes.

In recent years, homemakers have welcomed the additional features available on electric skillets. A broiling unit in the lid gives her a combination skillet and portable broiler when she purchases a broiler-frypan. The buffet skillet, a deep skillet with two carrying handles, often has a lid that can be propped open in different positions. Other features available include a non-stick lining, a removable thermostat, and a high dome lid.

Cleaning an electric skillet is easy if you follow these hints. Before washing the skillet, gently heat a soap and water solution in it then allow the skillet to soak. At dishwashing time, wash the skillet in soapy water remembering not to immerse the thermostat.

← **Fascinate guests** by skillfully using chopsticks to turn the meat for Oriental Chi Chow. Thin steak strips, crisp-cooked vegetables, peach slices, and a soy-flavored sauce merge in this exotic main dish.

ORIENTAL CHI CHOW

1 pound sirloin steak, 1 inch thick
2 tablespoons salad oil
1 pint fresh mushrooms, sliced
1 5-ounce can bamboo shoots, drained (⅔ cup)
1 5-ounce can water chestnuts, drained and sliced (⅔ cup)
1 medium onion, cut in wedges
½ cup sliced green onion
½ cup condensed beef broth
1 tablespoon sugar
. . .
2 teaspoons cornstarch
¼ cup soy sauce
1 tablespoon cold water
1 16-ounce can sliced peaches, drained
Ginger Rice

Partially freeze meat, then slice in thin strips. In skillet brown meat, half at a time, in hot salad oil. Add mushrooms, bamboo shoots, water chestnuts, onion, beef broth, and sugar. Cover; simmer 5 minutes.

Blend cornstarch, soy sauce, and water. Stir into meat mixture. Cook, stirring constantly, till thickened and bubbly. Add sliced peaches; cover and heat through. Serve over hot Ginger Rice. Makes 4 or 5 servings.

Ginger Rice: Mix 2 cups hot cooked rice with ½ teaspoon ground ginger.

WIENER SCHNITZEL

Cut 1½ pounds ½-inch-thick veal round steak *or* cutlets into 4 pieces; pound ¼ to ⅛ inch thick. Cut small slashes around edges to prevent curling. Combine ¼ cup all-purpose flour, 1 teaspoon salt, and ¼ teaspoon pepper. Coat meat with flour mixture. Combine 1 beaten egg and 1 tablespoon milk. Dip cutlets in egg mixture, then in 1 cup fine dry bread crumbs.

In skillet cook meat in ¼ cup hot salad oil for 2 to 3 minutes on each side, or till tender. Serve with lemon wedges. Makes 4 servings.

SUKIYAKI

        1 pound beef tenderloin, very
            thinly sliced across the grain
        2 tablespoons salad oil
        2 tablespoons sugar
      ½ cup beef stock *or* canned
            condensed beef broth
      ⅓ cup soy sauce
        2 cups bias-cut green onions
            cut 2 inches long
        1 cup bias-cut celery slices
            cut 1 inch long
        1 cup thinly sliced fresh mushrooms
        1 5-ounce can water chestnuts,
            drained and thinly sliced
        1 5-ounce can bamboo shoots,
            drained
        5 cups torn fresh spinach leaves
        1 16-ounce can bean sprouts,
            drained
      12 to 16 ounces bean curd,
            cubed* (optional)
        Hot cooked rice

In electric skillet brown beef quickly in hot oil for 1 to 2 minutes. Sprinkle with sugar. Combine stock and soy; pour over meat. Push meat to one side. Cook till soy mixture bubbles.

Keeping in separate groups, add onion and celery. Cook and toss-stir each group over high heat about 1 minute; push to one side. Again keeping in separate groups, add mushrooms, water chestnuts, bamboo shoots, spinach, bean sprouts, and bean curd. Cook and stir each food just till heated through. Serve with rice. Pass soy sauce, if desired. Serves 4.

*Bean curd (tofu) may be found at Japanese food shops or obtained from mail-order houses that specialize in Oriental foods.

DEVILED STEAK

Broil 1½ pounds sirloin steak till rare. In electric skillet combine 2 tablespoons butter, 1 tablespoon *each* snipped parsley and sherry, 1 teaspoon *each* dry mustard and Worcestershire sauce, ¼ teaspoon salt, and dash pepper; heat.

Add steak. Pour 2 tablespoons brandy over; ignite. When flames die, remove steak and cut into 6 pieces. Stir into sauce one 3-ounce can sliced mushrooms, drained, and ¼ cup catsup. Serve over steak. Makes 6 servings.

STUFFED HAM ROLLS

Served with a tangy pineapple sauce—

        1 20½-ounce can pineapple spears
        1 chicken bouillon cube
      ½ cup boiling water
        1 tablespoon butter or margarine
      ¼ cup chopped onion
      1½ cups herb-seasoned stuffing mix
        8 slices boiled ham
        2 tablespoons butter or margarine
                • • •
      ¼ cup sugar
        1 tablespoon cornstarch
        Dash salt
        1 beaten egg yolk

Drain pineapple, reserving 1 cup syrup; set aside. Dissolve bouillon cube in boiling water. In small skillet cook onion in the 1 tablespoon butter or margarine till tender; add stuffing mix and bouillon; stir to moisten.

Place 1 pineapple spear on a ham slice; spread with 3 tablespoons stuffing mixture. Roll up; secure with wooden pick. Repeat with remaining ham slices. Melt the 2 tablespoons butter or margarine in electric skillet. Add ham rolls; cook at 250° for 10 minutes or till heated through. Remove to hot serving platter.

Increase skillet temperature to 375°. Combine sugar, cornstarch, and salt; add reserved syrup. Stir into butter in skillet; cook and stir till mixture is thickened and bubbly. Gradually stir small amount of hot mixture into beaten egg yolk. Return to skillet; cook 1 minute more. Serve over ham rolls. Makes 4 servings.

HAM IN SOUR CREAM

In electric skillet melt ¼ cup butter or margarine. Add 2 cups fully-cooked ham cut in julienne strips and ½ cup finely chopped onion; cook till onion is tender but not brown. Add one 3-ounce can chopped mushrooms, drained, and 1 tablespoon chopped canned pimiento. Combine 2 cups dairy sour cream, ⅓ cup milk, and 1 tablespoon all-purpose flour; gradually stir into ham mixture.

Cook at 240°, stirring constantly, for 2 to 3 minutes or till mixture thickens (do not boil). Serve over hot cooked rice or cooked asparagus spears. Makes 6 to 8 servings.

CAULIFLOWER-HAM SALAD

Separate ½ medium head cauliflower into flow-erets; cook till crisp-tender. Drain and slice lengthwise. In electric skillet at 300° combine 2 tablespoons salad oil, 1 tablespoon sugar, 2 teaspoons cornstarch, 2 teaspoons instant minced onion, 1 teaspoon prepared mustard, ½ teaspoon garlic salt, ¼ teaspoon salt, and dash pepper. Blend in ⅔ cup water and ⅓ cup vinegar. Cook, stirring constantly, till mixture is thickened and bubbly.

Add cauliflower and 2 cups fully-cooked ham cut in 1½ inch strips; heat through. Toss with 6 cups torn lettuce, 1 cup halved cherry tomatoes, and ½ cup sliced celery. Cook 30 seconds longer. Serve immediately. Serves 8.

POTATO PANCAKES

Traditionally served with hot applesauce—

Cover 3 medium peeled potatoes with cold water; drain. Shred at once; drain off excess water (should have about 2½ cups potatoes).

In medium mixing bowl combine shredded potatoes; 2 slices bacon, crisp-cooked and crumbled (optional); 1 beaten egg; 1 tablespoon all-purpose flour; 1 tablespoon snipped parsley; 1 teaspoon grated onion; ¾ teaspoon salt; dash pepper; and dash grated nutmeg. Blend well.

In hot, greased electric skillet drop about ¼ cup batter for each pancake; flatten out evenly. Cook till brown, turning once, about 6 to 8 minutes. Makes 4 servings.

Spoon up generous helpings of Cauliflower Ham Salad for a taste-pleasing main dish. Julienne strips of ham, crisp-cooked cauliflower, lettuce, celery, and cherry tomatoes are tossed together with a steaming vinegar-oil dressing. The accompanying crispy corn-sticks are baked in corn ear-shaped molds.

TUNA PILAF

    1 3-ounce can sliced mushrooms,
        drained
    ¼ cup finely chopped onion
    ¼ cup finely chopped celery
    2 tablespoons finely chopped green
        pepper
    2 tablespoons butter or margarine
                • • •
    3 cups cooked rice
    1 6½- or 7-ounce can tuna, drained
    1 teaspoon Worcestershire sauce
    ½ teaspoon salt
    ⅛ teaspoon dried thyme leaves,
        crushed
      Dash pepper

Set electric skillet at 300°; in skillet cook mush-rooms, onion, celery, and green pepper in butter till tender. Add rice, tuna, Worcestershire sauce, salt, thyme, and pepper; toss to mix. Reduce heat to 200°; cook and stir till heated through. Makes 4 servings.

POTATO-FISH FILLETS

No need to serve potatoes with the meal—

    2 16-ounce packages frozen haddock
        fillets, thawed
    ½ teaspoon garlic salt
    ½ cup powdered packaged instant
        mashed potatoes
    3 tablespoons salad oil
                • • •
    1 13¾-ounce can chicken broth
        (1¾ cup)
    3 tablespoons powdered packaged
        instant mashed potatoes
    2 tablespoons finely chopped onion
    1 tablespoon lemon juice
    2 teaspoons dried parsley flakes

Separate fillets; cut into serving-size pieces. Sprinkle both sides with garlic salt. Roll fillets in the ½ cup instant mashed potatoes.

Set electric skillet at 380°; in skillet fry fish in hot oil till browned, turning once. Remove from skillet to warm serving platter. Combine remaining ingredients in skillet; simmer, stir-ring constantly, till thickened. Pass hot sauce with fish. Makes 6 to 8 servings.

LUNCHEON SHRIMP CURRY

    ¾ cup chopped onion
    ¾ cup chopped celery
    2 to 3 teaspoons curry powder
    ¼ cup butter or margarine
    2 10½-ounce cans condensed cream
        of celery soup
    1 16-ounce can applesauce (2 cups)
    1 pound shrimp, peeled, cleaned,
        and halved lengthwise
    1 3-ounce can sliced mushrooms,
        drained
      Hot cooked rice

Set electric skillet at 340°; in skillet cook onion, celery, and curry powder in butter till crisp-tender. Stir in soup, applesauce, shrimp, and mushrooms. Simmer, uncovered, 10 minutes; stir often. Serve over rice. Makes 8 servings.

MEAT AND YAM SKILLET

Cut one 12-ounce can luncheon meat in 8 slices; stud with whole cloves. In electric skillet brown meat on both sides in 1 tablespoon but-ter or margarine; push to one side of skillet.

Add one 16-ounce can sweet potatoes, drained; sprinkle sweet potatoes with salt. Spoon ⅓ cup peach *or* pineapple preserves over meat and potatoes. Heat, uncovered, over low heat; baste mixture often till hot and glazed, about 5 minutes. Makes 4 servings.

CHICKEN SCRAMBLE

    8 beaten eggs
    2 ounces *natural* Cheddar cheese,
        shredded (½ cup)
    ¼ cup milk
    ½ teaspoon salt
      Dash pepper
    3 tablespoons butter or margarine
    1 cup cooked chicken cut in
        julienne strips
    1 tablespoon snipped chives

In bowl combine first 5 ingredients. Set electric skillet at 320°; melt butter in skillet. Add chicken and chives; cook and stir 3 minutes. Add egg-cheese mixture. Cook, stirring occa-sionally, till eggs are set. Makes 6 servings.

SWEET-SOUR SHRIMP

3 tablespoons sugar
2 tablespoons cornstarch
1 cup chicken broth
⅔ cup pineapple juice
¼ cup vinegar
2 tablespoons soy sauce
1 tablespoon butter or margarine

. . .

1 7-ounce package frozen Chinese
   pea pods, thawed
2 4½-ounce cans shrimp, drained
2 to 2½ cups hot cooked rice

In electric skillet blend sugar and cornstarch; stir in chicken broth. Add pineapple juice, vinegar, soy sauce, and butter or margarine. Cook, stirring constantly, till mixture thickens and bubbles. Cover and simmer 5 minutes longer. Stir in Chinese pea pods and drained shrimp; heat through. Serve shrimp mixture over hot cooked rice. Makes 4 or 5 servings.

TURKEY HASH

Makes good use of leftover turkey—

¼ cup butter or margarine
3 cups finely chopped raw potatoes
   (about 3 medium potatoes)
3 cups finely chopped turkey
¼ cup chopped onion
¼ cup chopped green pepper
1 10½-ounce can chicken gravy
   (1¼ cups)
1 cup water
¼ teaspoon salt
   Dash dried rosemary leaves,
   crushed
   Dash pepper

. . .

Green pepper rings

Set electric skillet at 200°; melt butter or margarine in skillet. Add potatoes, turkey, onion, chopped green pepper, chicken gravy, water, salt, rosemary, and pepper; mix well.

Cover; simmer mixture for 15 minutes or till vegetables are tender, stirring occasionally. Add small amount of additional water, if needed. Garnish hash with green pepper rings. Serve hot. Makes 4 servings.

CURRIED SHRIMP SKILLET

Oriental flavor added to macaroni-cheese mix—

2 tablespoons butter or margarine
1 medium apple, peeled and chopped
   (1 cup)
½ cup sliced celery
¾ teaspoon curry powder

. . .

1 chicken bouillon cube
2 cups water
1 7¼-ounce package macaroni and
   cheese mix
½ teaspoon salt
¾ cup milk
1 4½-ounce can shrimp, drained

Melt butter or margarine in electric skillet. Add chopped apple, sliced celery, and curry powder; cook till crisp-tender. Reduce heat; add bouillon cube, water, macaroni from packaged mix, and salt. Cover skillet. Cook over medium heat till macaroni is tender, about 6 to 7 minutes, stirring occasionally.

Stir in milk and cheese from packaged mix. Top macaroni-cheese mixture with drained shrimp. Heat through. Makes 4 servings.

QUICK APPLE DUMPLINGS

Spicy apple dumplings become a quick and tasty dessert with the use of convenience foods—

1 21-ounce can apple pie filling
2½ cups water
½ cup raisins
⅓ cup red cinnamon candies
⅓ cup sugar
¼ cup chopped nuts
2 tablespoons butter or margarine
1 tablespoon lemon juice

. . .

1 package refrigerated cinnamon
   rolls with icing (8 rolls)

In electric skillet combine all ingredients *except* rolls. Cook and stir till butter melts and mixture is bubbly. Arrange rolls atop filling. Cover; with lid vent open cook at 250° for 20 to 25 minutes or till rolls are done. Spread icing from package over rolls. Serve warm with cream, if desired. Makes 8 servings.

A JAPANESE SPECIALTY

Add a far-eastern flavor to dining with Japanese Tempura—batter-dipped shrimp and vegetables deep-fat fried in an electric skillet. Begin the adventure with Chawan-Mushi (Japanese Custard Soup) followed with tempura and rice. Fruit, tea, and sake complete the culinary visit.

MENU

Japanese Custard Soup
Japanese Tempura
Hot Cooked Rice
Fresh Fruit

Sake   *Tea*

Guests will enjoy dining at a low table accompanied with plenty of soft floor pillows. (Plan on no more than 6 to 8 people.) Arrange a black or brightly-colored lacquered tray at each place setting—they need not match—or, use bamboo place mats. Chopsticks add authenticity, although it is wise to furnish knives, forks, and spoons. Provide small cups for warm sake (rice wine). Attractively arranged fresh fruit can double as the centerpiece and dessert. Set an electric skillet adjacent to your place setting for the tempura. Just before cooking tempura, blend premeasured ingredients and add ice cubes to thoroughly chill the batter. Using one set of tongs for dipping and another set for frying, cook only a few of the batter-coated pieces at a time. When golden brown, drain them while piping hot. Pass tempura condiments with the crispy shrimp and vegetables.

Following dessert, let guests linger over hot tea. Served at a leisurely pace, Japanese-style dining allows each diner to enjoy the conversation as well as the food.

← **Fresh vegetables and shrimp** cooked in Japanese Tempura are a crisp delicacy served from the electric skillet. To eat, dip in condiments: mustard sauce, gingerroot, or a mixture of radish and turnip.

JAPANESE CUSTARD SOUP

6 raw shrimp, peeled and cleaned
6 spinach leaves, cut in 1½-inch pieces
⅓ cup sliced fresh mushrooms
6 water chestnuts, sliced
2 slightly beaten eggs
1 13¾-ounce can chicken broth

Make small slit in each shrimp; pull tail through. Pour hot water over spinach to wilt; drain. Divide and arrange shrimp, spinach, mushrooms, and water chestnuts in six 5-ounce custard cups *or* Chawan-Mushi cups.

Combine eggs, broth, and ½ teaspoon salt; pour into cups. Cover cups with foil; set on wire rack in Dutch oven. Pour hot water around cups 1 inch deep; cover kettle. Over medium heat bring water to simmering. Reduce heat; cook 10 minutes or till knife inserted halfway between center and edge comes out clean.

Top each custard with ¼ teaspoon soy sauce and twist of lemon peel, if desired. Serves 6.

JAPANESE TEMPURA

Raw shrimp, peeled and cleaned
Assorted fresh vegetables such as asparagus spears, parsley, sweet potatoes, spinach, mushrooms, and green beans
Salad oil
1 cup sifted all-purpose flour
1 cup ice water
1 slightly beaten egg
2 tablespoons salad oil
½ teaspoon sugar
Tempura Condiments

Wash and dry shrimp and vegetables well. Slice or cut vegetables into strips, if necessary. Fill skillet ½ full with salad oil; heat to 360° to 365°. To make batter combine flour, next 4 ingredients, and ½ teaspoon salt; beat just till moistened—a few lumps should remain. Stir in one or two ice cubes. Use immediately.

Dip shrimp and vegetables in cold batter. Fry in hot oil till light brown; drain.

Serve with Tempura Condiments: 1. grated fresh gingerroot; 2. equal parts grated turnip and radish, combined; and 3. ½ cup prepared mustard mixed with 3 tablespoons soy sauce.

JUST FOR THE FAMILY

Next time the whole family is home for a relaxed meal, make the most of the occasion by serving this mouth-watering menu. Glamorize the ground beef patties with a sweet-sour sauce, and add a tossed salad and hash-brown potatoes. The meal highlight is the electric skillet dessert of fluffy dumplings cooked at the table in a strawberry-orange sauce.

MENU

Sweet-Sour Burgers
Tossed Salad   *French Dressing*
Hash-Browns
Strawberry Dumplings
Beverage

Even though this home-style menu doesn't require the best china and silver, don't neglect the table setting. For an attractive setting, use a bright colored cloth, an informal flower arrangement for a centerpiece, and set the table neatly with everyday tableware.

To avoid spending last-minute time in the kitchen, prepare the strawberry sauce and dumpling batter separately; cook the dumplings right at the table. Drop the batter into the gently bubbling sauce about 15 minutes before it's time for dessert. Cover the skillet and don't peek until the dumplings are done. Spoon some warm sauce over each serving, then pass the cream and start accepting the compliments.

HASH-BROWNS

Boil 4 medium potatoes in jackets; chill. Peel and shred to make 4 cups. Add 1 to 2 tablespoons grated onion, 1 teaspoon salt, and dash pepper. In 10-inch skillet melt ⅓ cup butter or margarine. Pat potatoes into pan, leaving ½-inch space around edge. Brown 10 to 12 minutes. Reduce heat if necessary. Cut with spatula to make 6 wedges; turn. Brown 8 to 10 minutes longer or till golden. Makes 6 servings.

SWEET-SOUR BURGERS

  1 8-ounce can tomato sauce (1 cup)
  6 gingersnaps, crushed (⅓ cup)
 ⅓ cup finely chopped onion
 ¼ cup raisins
  1 beaten egg
1½ pounds ground beef
  2 tablespoons brown sugar
  1 tablespoon vinegar
  1 teaspoon prepared mustard

Combine ¼ *cup* of the tomato sauce, the gingersnaps, onion, raisins, egg, and ¾ teaspoon salt. Add meat; mix well. Shape into six patties; brown in skillet. Combine the remaining tomato sauce, the brown sugar, vinegar, mustard, and dash pepper; pour over burgers. Cover and simmer 20 minutes, spooning sauce over burgers occasionally. Makes 6 servings.

STRAWBERRY DUMPLINGS

  1 21-ounce can strawberry pie
     filling
1½ cups orange juice
  1 cup water
 ¼ cup sugar
  1 tablespoon butter or margarine
     Few drops red food coloring
1½ cups sifted all-purpose flour
 ⅓ cup sugar
  1 tablespoon baking powder
 ⅔ cup milk
  2 tablespoons salad oil
     Ground cinnamon *or* nutmeg

In electric skillet combine first 5 ingredients. Heat to boiling. Add red food coloring. In mixing bowl sift together flour, the ⅓ cup sugar, baking powder, and ½ teaspoon salt. Stir in milk and oil. Drop in 6 portions onto boiling fruit mixture. Sprinkle lightly with cinnamon or nutmeg. Cover; cook at 200° for 10 to 12 minutes or till dumplings are done. Serve warm with cream, if desired. Makes 6 servings.

Bright red strawberries adorn the top of these →
Strawberry Dumplings. The fluffy dumplings are served hot from the electric skillet as the finale of a family-pleasing dinner. Serve with cream, if desired.

WAFFLES THAT BAKE WHERE YOU EAT

Start the day with piping hot waffles for breakfast or wind it up with an ice cream-topped waffle dessert after the theater. In between are occasions for sophisticated waffle entrees served with a cheese, meat, or seafood sauce. Different flavored waffles are possible with the addition of fruit, nuts, chocolate, and other ingredients. Often served with maple syrup, waffles are also delicious topped with fruit-flavored syrups or fresh or canned fruit sauces.

It is no wonder that waffle bakers are a popular appliance. They are easy to use and convenient for cooking at the table. Available in round, square, or oblong styles, waffle bakers may be purchased in various sizes to accommodate family needs. Some are equipped with interchangeable grids for baking waffles with novelty designs. Others have grids which convert the appliance into a grill.

LOBSTER-CHEESE WAFFLES

      1¼ cups sifted all-purpose flour
       2 teaspoons baking powder
       1 teaspoon sugar
      ¼ teaspoon salt
       2 ounces sharp process American
          cheese, shredded (½ cup)
       1 beaten egg
      1¼ cups milk
      ¼ cup salad oil
          Lobster Sauce

Sift together first 4 ingredients; stir in cheese. Combine egg, milk, and oil; add to dry ingredients, mixing only till dry ingredients are moistened. Bake in preheated waffle baker. Serve with Lobster Sauce. Makes 4 servings.

Lobster Sauce: In saucepan melt 2 tablespoons butter. Blend in 2 tablespoons all-purpose flour and ¼ teaspoon salt. Add 1½ cups milk. Cook and stir till thickened and bubbly. Remove from heat. Add 2 ounces sharp process American cheese, shredded (½ cup); stir till melted. Stir in one 5-ounce can lobster, drained, flaked, and cartilage removed, and 1 teaspoon lemon juice. Reheat just to boiling.

BASIC WAFFLES

Sift together 1¾ cups sifted all-purpose flour, 3 teaspoons baking powder, and ½ teaspoon salt. Combine 2 beaten egg yolks, 1¾ cups milk, and ½ cup salad oil *or* melted shortening; stir into dry ingredients. Fold in 2 stiffly beaten egg whites, leaving a few fluffs. Bake in preheated waffle baker. Serves 4 to 6.

WAFFLED EGGWICHES

Combine 4 hard-cooked eggs, chopped; ⅓ cup mayonnaise; ¼ cup chopped celery; 2 tablespoons drained sweet pickle relish; 2 tablespoons snipped parsley; ½ teaspoon salt; ¼ teaspoon dry mustard; and dash pepper.

Spread egg filling on 4 slices white bread; top with 4 more slices white bread. Spread outside surfaces of sandwiches with ¼ cup softened butter or margarine. Bake sandwiches in preheated waffle baker till golden. Serve immediately. Makes 4 servings.

TUNA-SAUCED WAFFLES

      ⅔ cup milk
       2 tablespoons salad oil
       1 well-beaten egg
       1 cup packaged biscuit mix
          Creamy Tuna Sauce

Combine milk, oil, and egg. Stir into biscuit mix; mix well. Bake in preheated waffle baker. Serve with Creamy Tuna Sauce. Serves 4 to 6.

Creamy Tuna Sauce: Cook 2 tablespoons finely chopped onion in 2 tablespoons butter till tender but not brown; add ¼ cup green pepper strips, cut 1 inch long. Cook 1 minute more. Stir in one 10½-ounce can condensed cream of mushroom soup; one 7-ounce can chunk-style tuna, drained and broken up; one 3-ounce can chopped mushrooms, drained; and ½ cup milk. Heat just to boiling; stir occasionally. Serve over waffles. Sprinkle each serving with process American cheese, shredded, if desired.

Delectable Chocolate Dot Waffles are prepared with semisweet chocolate pieces sprinkled atop each waffle before baking. Served for brunch or dessert, they are delicious topped with a mound of whipped cream and shredded orange peel. For convenience, bake at the table and serve hot from the waffle baker.

CHOCOLATE DOT WAFFLES

Sift together 2¼ cups sifted all-purpose flour, 1½ tablespoons sugar, 4 teaspoons baking powder, and ¾ teaspoon salt. In mixing bowl combine 2¼ cups milk, 2 beaten eggs, and ½ cup salad oil. Add liquid mixture to sifted dry ingredients just before baking waffles, beating only till dry ingredients are moistened. (This waffle batter will be thin.)

Pour some batter onto preheated waffle baker. Using one 6-ounce package semisweet chocolate pieces (1 cup), sprinkle each unbaked waffle with a few chocolate pieces. Bake waffles.

For each serving top 2 waffles with a dollop of whipped cream and sprinkle with shredded orange peel. Makes 4 servings.

GINGERETTES

    3 cups gingersnap crumbs
        (45 cookies)
    4 teaspoons baking powder
    1 cup milk
    3 beaten egg yolks
    ¼ cup butter, melted
    3 stiffly beaten egg whites
        Vanilla ice cream
        Sliced peaches, sweetened

Combine crumbs, baking powder, and ½ teaspoon salt. Mix milk, yolks, and butter; stir into crumbs. Fold in whites. (Do not overmix.) Bake in preheated waffle baker. Top with ice cream and peaches. Makes 8 servings.

WAFFLES FOR BREAKFAST

On one of those brisk fall or winter mornings when just anticipating the chilly weather makes the family hungry, serve a warm-up breakfast featuring Waffles with Toppers.

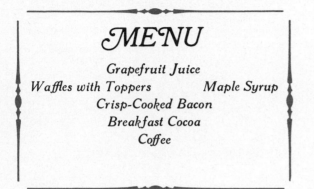

MENU

Grapefruit Juice
Waffles with Toppers   Maple Syrup
Crisp-Cooked Bacon
Breakfast Cocoa
Coffee

The family won't want to wait for breakfast on a cold morning so be a few steps ahead by starting the night before. Make the syrup and put the juice in refrigerator to chill. Measure and combine dry ingredients for cocoa and waffles. Nut and coconut condiments and syrup are made ready in serving containers. Place settings and appliances can be arranged, too.

In the morning start the coffee, prepare the apple chunks, and fry the bacon. Meanwhile, preheat the waffle baker at the table. The cocoa is heated while you mix the waffle batter.

As the aroma of breakfast cooking gathers the family around the table, bring on the food and start baking the waffles. Now, just try to stay ahead of the enthusiastic breakfasters.

MAPLE SYRUP

In small saucepan combine 1 cup light corn syrup, ½ cup brown sugar, and ½ cup water; cook, stirring constantly, till sugar is dissolved. Add 1 tablespoon butter or margarine and dash maple flavoring. Makes about 1½ cups.

← **Dress up everyday waffles** by serving Waffles with Toppers. Just before baking sprinkle batter with apple, pecan, or coconut-orange peel topping. Drizzle homemade Maple Syrup over the golden waffles.

WAFFLES WITH TOPPERS

Also great for brunch or Sunday supper—

2¼ cups sifted all-purpose flour
1½ tablespoons sugar
4 teaspoons baking powder
¾ teaspoon salt
2¼ cups milk
2 beaten eggs
½ cup salad oil
· · ·
2 tablespoons flaked coconut
1 tablespoon shredded orange peel
¼ cup diced unpeeled apple
1 teaspoon sugar
Few dashes ground nutmeg
¼ cup chopped pecans

In mixing bowl sift together flour, the 1½ tablespoons sugar, baking powder, and salt. Combine milk, eggs, and salad oil. Add to dry ingredients just before baking, mixing only till dry ingredients are moistened. (Batter is thin.)

In small bowl combine coconut and shredded orange peel. In another bowl combine diced apple, the 1 teaspoon sugar, and the nutmeg.

Pour batter onto preheated waffle baker; quickly top with a small amount of coconut-orange peel mixture, apple, or pecans. Bake. Serve with butter and maple-flavored syrup, if desired. Makes 10 to 12 waffles.

BREAKFAST COCOA

Capped with a dollop of marshmallow creme—

⅓ cup unsweetened cocoa powder
⅓ cup sugar
Dash salt
½ cup water
· · ·
3½ cups milk
½ teaspoon vanilla
Marshmallow creme

In a saucepan mix unsweetened cocoa powder, sugar, and salt; add water. Bring to boiling, stirring constantly. Boil 1 minute. Stir in milk; heat almost to boiling (do not boil). Add vanilla; beat with rotary beater just before serving. Float dollops of marshmallow creme atop each serving. Makes 4 cups.

GRIDDLE SPECIALTIES

Cooking breakfast at the table is easy when you use a griddle. Since several foods can be grilled at one time, quick-cooking meats, eggs, French toast, and pancakes are done in little time. When you've finished, just wipe cooled griddle with paper toweling to remove excess grease, then wash in hot, soapy water.

This method of cooking is great for sandwiches browned on both sides in a small amount of fat. For a crunchier crust, dip sandwiches in an egg mixture and coat with crumbs before grilling. Served hot, they provide an excellent lunch or evening snack accompanied with soup, relishes, and/or fruit.

You can even grill fruits and vegetables— pineapple slices, peach halves, tomato halves, or onion slices. Delicious as a meat accompaniment, they can be placed on the grill alongside the meat the last few minutes of cooking.

Available in many attractive designs, electric griddles are also convenient for serving at the table or on the patio. Those equipped with a very low temperature setting can double as a food warmer. When entertaining, they are ideal for serving hot appetizers or keeping food hot on the buffet table.

CRUNCHY HAM SANDWICHES

> 8 **slices white bread**
> **Butter or margarine, softened**
> **Prepared mustard**
> 4 **slices boiled ham**
> 4 **slices process American cheese**
> 1 **tomato, thinly sliced**
> • • •
> 2 **slightly beaten eggs**
> 2 **tablespoons milk**
> **Dash onion salt**
> • • •
> 1¼ **cups crushed potato chips**

Spread 4 slices bread on one side with butter; spread remaining bread slices on one side with mustard. Top each mustard-spread slice with 1 slice ham, 1 slice cheese, 1 or 2 tomato slices, then second slice of bread, buttered side down.

Combine eggs, milk, and onion salt. Dip sandwiches in egg mixture, then in crushed potato chips. Pat to secure chips to bread, turning to coat both sides. Brown on medium-hot, lightly greased griddle till crisp, about 8 minutes, turning once. Makes 4 servings.

TUNA-BERRY SANDWICHES

> 1 **6½- or 7-ounce can tuna, drained and flaked**
> ¼ **cup finely chopped celery**
> 2 **tablespoons chopped walnuts**
> ¼ **cup mayonnaise or salad dressing**
> 8 **slices white bread**
> 1 **8-ounce can jellied cranberry sauce, sliced ¼ inch thick**
> • • •
> 2 **slightly beaten eggs**
> 3 **tablespoons milk**
> **Dash salt**

Combine tuna, celery, nuts, and mayonnaise. Spread filling on 4 slices bread. Arrange cranberry slices atop filling; top with remaining bread. Combine eggs, milk, and salt. Dip sandwiches in egg mixture. Brown on medium-hot, lightly greased griddle, about 6 to 8 minutes, turning once. Makes 4 servings.

TURKEY DOUBLE-DECKER

> 18 **slices rye bread**
> **Mayonnaise or salad dressing**
> 6 **slices process Swiss cheese**
> 1½ **cups finely chopped cabbage**
> 6 **slices boiled ham**
> **Mayonnaise or salad dressing**
> 6 **slices cooked turkey**
> **Butter or margarine, softened**

Spread one side of each slice bread with mayonnaise. On *each* of 6 slices bread stack 1 slice cheese, about 2 tablespoons cabbage, and 1 slice ham. Cover with second slice bread, mayonnaise-side down; spread top side with mayonnaise. Cover with 1 slice turkey, about 2 tablespoons cabbage, and third slice bread.

Spread top of sandwiches with butter. Place on medium-hot griddle, buttered side down. Spread top slices with butter. Grill till browned, about 12 to 15 minutes, turning once. Serves 6.

Crushed potato chips make Crunchy Ham Sandwiches a grill favorite easily prepared on short notice. Crushed chips cling to egg-coated sandwiches that are packed with slices of ham, cheese, and tomato. Offer crisp relishes and beverage to complete the meal. For heartier appetites, add hot soup and dessert.

GERMAN SANDWICHES

  ¼ cup butter, softened
  2 tablespoons prepared horseradish
     mustard
  2 tablespoons finely chopped onion
  2 teaspoons poppy seed
  8 slices rye bread
  4 slices boiled ham
  4 slices process Swiss cheese

Combine first 4 ingredients; spread butter mixture on both sides of each bread slice. Top each of 4 slices bread with 1 slice ham, 1 slice cheese, then second slice of bread. Brown on medium-hot griddle till cheese melts, about 10 minutes, turning once. Makes 4 servings.

GRILLED BEEFWICHES

  1 tablespoon dry onion soup mix
  1 tablespoon prepared horseradish
    Dash pepper
  6 tablespoons butter, softened
  8 slices white bread
  8 thin slices cooked roast beef
  4 slices process Swiss cheese

Soften soup mix in 1 tablespoon water. Stir soup mix, horseradish, and pepper into butter. Spread on both sides of each slice bread. Top each of 4 slices bread with 2 slices beef, 1 slice cheese, then second slice of bread. Brown sandwiches on medium-hot griddle till cheese melts, about 10 minutes, turning once. Serves 4.

GRILLED SALMONWICHES

Dipped in egg batter just before grilling—

- 1 7¾-ounce can salmon
- ⅓ cup milk
- 2 well-beaten eggs
  Dash ground nutmeg
- ¼ cup finely chopped celery
- ¼ cup dairy sour cream
- 1 teaspoon prepared horseradish
- 1 teaspoon prepared mustard
- ½ teaspoon finely chopped green onion
- ¼ teaspoon dried tarragon leaves, crushed
- 8 slices bread
  Sesame seed

Drain salmon, reserving liquid. Remove bones and skin from salmon; flake meat into bowl. In shallow dish combine salmon liquid, milk, eggs, and nutmeg. Blend together salmon, celery, sour cream, horseradish, mustard, onion, ¼ teaspoon salt, tarragon, and dash pepper. Spread mixture evenly on 4 slices bread; top with the remaining bread slices.

Dip each sandwich into egg mixture; sprinkle with sesame seed. Cook on hot, lightly greased griddle, browning on both sides. Serves 4.

SAUCY EGG PATTIES

Using one 10½-ounce can condensed cream of shrimp soup, combine ¼ *cup* soup (set aside remainder for sauce) with 8 chopped hard-cooked eggs; ¼ cup fine dry bread crumbs; 2 tablespoons milk; 1 tablespoon snipped parsley; 2 teaspoons finely chopped onion; ¼ teaspoon salt; and dash pepper. Form mixture into 8 patties. Coat patties with ½ cup fine dry bread crumbs. On hot, lightly greased griddle cook patties till golden, turning to brown both sides. Combine remaining soup, 3 tablespoons milk, and ¼ teaspoon curry powder in saucepan; heat. Pass with patties. Serves 4.

←**Pineapple-studded fruit sauce** drizzles down sides of light-as-a-feather Hawaiian Pancakes—an imaginative entree at brunch. For a luscious dessert, garnish each serving with whipped cream.

HAWAIIAN PANCAKES

- 1 20½-ounce can pineapple tidbits
- 2 tablespoons cornstarch
- ⅓ cup orange juice
- ⅓ cup honey
- 2 tablespoons butter or margarine
- 2 cups sifted all-purpose flour
- ¼ cup sugar
- 4 tablespoons baking powder
- 2 cups milk
- 2 beaten eggs
- ¼ cup salad oil

Drain pineapple, reserving syrup; add enough water to syrup to make 1 cup. In saucepan blend syrup and cornstarch; add pineapple, orange juice, honey, and butter. Bring to boiling, stirring constantly. Keep warm.

Meanwhile, sift together flour, sugar, baking powder, and 1 teaspoon salt. Combine milk, eggs, and salad oil; add dry ingredients, beating till smooth. Using ¼ to ⅓ cup batter for each pancake bake on hot, lightly greased griddle till golden, turning once. Serve with pineapple sauce. Makes 4 to 6 servings.

PANCAKES A LA MODE

Good with applesauce and whipped cream, too—

- 1¼ cups sifted all-purpose flour
- ¾ teaspoon baking soda
- ½ teaspoon ground cinnamon
- ½ teaspoon ground ginger
- ¼ teaspoon ground nutmeg
- ½ cup light molasses
- ¼ cup butter or margarine, melted
- 1 slightly beaten egg
  Vanilla ice cream
  Maple-flavored syrup
  Chopped pecans

Sift together first 5 ingredients and ¼ teaspoon salt. Combine ⅔ cup water, molasses, butter, and egg; gradually add molasses mixture to flour mixture, blending just till smooth.

Using 2 tablespoons batter for each pancake, bake on medium-hot, lightly greased griddle for 3 to 4 minutes, turning once. Overlap two pancakes on each plate; top with scoop of ice cream, then syrup and nuts. Serves 6 to 8.

MEAL-ON-A-GRIDDLE

Spring is here and summer is just around the corner, so celebrate the arrival of beautiful weather with a griddle-meal on the patio. Remember though, that since the griddle is electric you'll need an electric outlet close by.

MENU

Saucy Steak Sandwich
Grilled Onions
Tossed Salad   Italian Parmesan Dressing
Glorified Rice
Iced Tea

This festive occasion deserves cheerful table decorations. Center the table with an old-fashioned coffeepot holding an arrangement of daisies. A pastel yellow cloth and napkins provide a splash of sunshine.

Spring is no time to spend hours in the kitchen so make every minute count. The dessert can be prepared the day before or early in the day, then chilled in individual sherbet dishes. Prepare the salad dressing and vegetables separately and toss together at the last minute. Just before serving time, make the tomato sauce for the sandwich and serve while still warm. The steak and thick slices of onion sprinkled with paprika are grilled at the table. Let everyone make his own sandwich by dipping toasted bread in tomato sauce and topping with steak hot off the griddle, then leisurely enjoy the good food and sunshine.

ITALIAN PARMESAN DRESSING

In screw-top jar combine 1⅓ cups salad oil; ½ cup vinegar; ¼ cup grated Parmesan cheese; 1 tablespoon sugar; 2 teaspoons salt; 1 teaspoon celery salt; ½ teaspoon white pepper; ½ teaspoon dry mustard; ¼ teaspoon paprika; and 1 clove garlic, minced. Cover and shake vigorously. Refrigerate till serving time. Shake again before serving. Makes 1¾ cups.

SAUCY STEAK SANDWICH

    1 8-ounce can tomato sauce
    ⅓ cup bottled steak sauce
    2 tablespoons brown sugar
    1 tablespoon salad oil
            • • •
    6 slices French bread, cut 1
        inch thick
    1 pound round steak, cut ¼ inch
        thick
    Instant meat tenderizer

To prepare sauce combine tomato sauce, steak sauce, brown sugar, and salad oil in small saucepan. Bring to boiling. Keep warm.

Toast the slices of French bread on both sides. Cut round steak into 6 pieces. Apply instant meat tenderizer according to label directions. Preheat griddle to 400°; grease lightly. Grill meat 2 to 3 minutes on each side. Sprinkle with pepper. To serve, dip slice of toast quickly into sauce; top with steak. Spoon on additional sauce. Makes 6 servings.

GLORIFIED RICE

    1 8¾-ounce can crushed pineapple
    ⅔ cup packaged precooked rice
    ½ teaspoon salt
    2 teaspoons lemon juice
            • • •
    1½ cups miniature marshmallows
    1 ripe banana, sliced
    1 cup whipping cream
    2 tablespoons chopped maraschino
        cherries

Drain pineapple, reserving syrup. In saucepan combine uncooked rice, ⅔ cup water, reserved syrup, and salt. Stir to moisten rice. Bring quickly to boil. Cover and simmer 5 minutes.

Remove from heat; let stand 5 minutes. Add pineapple and lemon juice; cool. Stir in marshmallows and banana. Whip cream. Fold cream and cherries into mixture; chill. Serves 6 to 8.

Sizzling steak and spicy tomato sauce atop a thick ➙ slice of toasted French bread make up this man-size Saucy Steak Sandwich. Paprika-sprinkled grilled onions and steak cook side-by-side on electric griddle.

DOUBLE CORN CAKES

Stir together 1 cup packaged pancake mix and 1 cup cornmeal. Combine one 16-ounce can cream-style corn, 1 cup milk, 2 slightly beaten eggs, and 2 tablespoons salad oil; add to flour mixture, stirring just till moistened.

Drop batter from ¼ cup measure onto hot, lightly greased griddle. Cook till browned, turning once. Makes sixteen 4-inch pancakes.

CUSTARD FRENCH TOAST

    ¼ cup all-purpose flour
    1 tablespoon sugar
    ½ teaspoon baking powder
    ⅛ teaspoon ground nutmeg
    1 cup milk
    3 slightly beaten eggs
    4 slices French bread, cut
        1 inch thick
        Maple-flavored syrup

Combine first 4 ingredients and ½ teaspoon salt. Mix milk with eggs; add flour mixture. Beat till smooth. Pour into shallow pan. Soak bread in egg mixture 15 minutes; turn carefully. Making sure both surfaces are thoroughly coated, soak 15 minutes more.

Fry bread slowly on medium-hot, lightly greased griddle till browned, about 20 minutes, turning once. Serve with syrup. Serves 4.

CHICKEN EGG FOO YONG

Combine ¾ cup finely chopped chicken *or* turkey, ⅓ cup finely chopped celery, ¼ cup finely chopped green pepper, ¼ cup finely chopped mushrooms, ¼ cup finely chopped water chestnuts, ½ teaspoon salt, and dash pepper. Add mixture to 6 well-beaten eggs; mix well.

Making 6 patties pour mixture onto hot, well-greased griddle. Shape with pancake turner by pushing egg back into patties. When set and brown on one side, turn to brown other side. Serve with Chinese Brown Sauce. Serves 3.

Chinese Brown Sauce: Melt 1 tablespoon butter or margarine. Combine 2 teaspoons cornstarch and 1 teaspoon sugar; blend into butter. Add ½ cup water and 1½ tablespoons soy sauce. Cook, stirring constantly, till mixture is thickened and bubbly.

TABLETOP APPLIANCES

Several hints will help you make the most of tabletop appliances. First, keep them handy by storing them within easy reach. Second, read instruction booklets for the helpful use and care tips that are included. And third, use them often to save time, becoming acquainted with all they can do (see picture, pages 66-67).

1. Electric barrel brazier with rotisserie
2. Electric deep-fat fryer—french-fried potatoes and onion rings, doughnuts, fritters, tempura, deep-fat fried meats
3. Hot tray and serving cart—keeps all foods warm at buffet or table-side
4. Electric skillet
5. Automatic toaster—breads, toaster pastries, nut breads, English muffins, waffles
6. Blender—beverages (cocktails, coolers, fruit juices, shakes), quick desserts, dips
7. Automatic bacon cooker—bacon, cold cuts
8. Covered portable charcoal cooker
9. Electric portable oven
10. Automatic egg cooker—soft-cooked, hard-cooked, or poached eggs
11. Automatic coffee maker—hot beverages
12. Cold server tray—keeps appetizers, salads, beverages, and desserts cold
13. French bread warmer—French bread, rolls
14. Automatic popcorn popper
15. Portable butane burner
16. Automatic hot pot—hot water, milk, soups, hot beverages
17. Electric waffle baker
18. Electric griddle
19. Electric hot plate

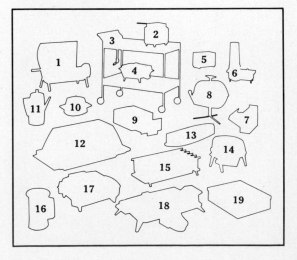

INDEX

A-B

Anchovy Butter, 20
Appetizers, *see also*
  Dip and Soup
  Bacon-Wrapped
    Chicken, 9
  Cider Snap, 47
  Cocktail
    Meatballs, 8
  Crab-Potato
    Nibblers, 8
  Crab-Stuffed
    Mushrooms, 48
  Cranberry-Sauced
    Bites, 44
  Crusty Vegetable
    Bites, 9
  French-Fried
    Cheese, 12
  Fruited Ham
    Balls, 8
  Hot Tomato
    Cocktail, 47
  Lemony-Shrimp
    Kabobs, 68
  Mapled, 48
  Meatballs,
    Spicy, 38
  Reuben, 8
  Saucy Sausages, 48
  Seafood in Wine, 48
  Strawberry
    Starter, 57
  Sweet-Sour
    Surprises, 49
  Teriyaki, 68
  Tiny Pronto Pups, 9
Apple Dumplings,
  Quick, 77
Apricot Crepes,
  Ham-, 54
Asparagus-Cheese
  Soup, 47
Avocado Dip,
  Sausage-, 10
Avocado Sauce,
  Creamy, 22
Bacon
  Dip, Cheese-, 44

Bacon *continued*
  Scramble,
    Noodle-, 54
  -Wrapped
    Chicken, 9
Bananas, Sauteed, 61
Basic Waffles, 82
Basil Butter, 20
Bean Dunk, Cheese
  and, 10
Bearnaise Sauce, 19
Beef
  Bites, Jazzy, 18
  Burgundied
    Tenderloin, 53
  -Cauliflower
    Combo, 70
  Deviled Steak, 74
  Fondue, 15
  Fondued Flank
    Steak, 16
  Fruit Kabobs,
    and, 68
  Saucy Steak
    Sandwich, 90
  Steak Diane, 58
  Stroganoff,
    Beer, 52
  Stroganoff,
    Classic, 52
  Sukiyaki, 74
  Teriyaki
    Appetizers, 68
  Beefwiches,
    Grilled, 87
Beer Beef
  Stroganoff, 52
Beer Cheese
  Fondue, 29
Berry Sandwiches,
  Tuna-, 86
Beverage
  Breakfast Cocoa, 85
  Cafe Brulot, 63
  Cider Snap, 47
  Daiquiri Blazer, 63
  Hot Tomato
    Cocktail, 47
  Mexican
    Chocolate, 23

Blueberry
  Dumplings, 62
Bordelaise Sauce, 19
Burgundied
  Tenderloin, 53
Butter
  Anchovy, 20
  Basil, 20
  Garlic, 20
Buttermilk
  Fondue, 28
Butterscotch
  Fondue, 36
Butterscotch-Nut
  Sauce, 63

C

Caesar Salad,
  Original, 58
Cafe Brulot, 63
Cake Cubes, Ice
  Cream-and-, 37
Cake, Pineapple
  Delight, 31
Cantonese Shrimp, 70
Caper Sauce, 21
Caramel Fondue, 36
Caraway-Cheese
  Fondue, 28
Catsup Sauce,
  Creamy, 19
Cauliflower
  Bowl, Tangy, 64
  Combo, Beef-, 70
  -Ham Salad, 75
Cheese
  -Bacon Dip, 44
  Bean Dunk, and, 10
  Dip, Chili con, 46
  Dip, Crab-, 46
  Dip, Deviled, 44
  Dip, Duo, 46
  -Filled Pears, 62
  Fondues, 26-33
  French-Fried, 12
  Sauce, Chili-, 22
  Soup,
    Asparagus-, 47
  -Sour Cream
    Fondue, 29
  Waffles,
    Lobster-, 82

Cheese Fondue
  Beer, 29
  Buttermilk, 28
  Caraway-, 28
  Classic, 26
  Cottage Swiss, 28
  Crab-, 28
  Creamy
    Parmesan, 29
  Dippers, 26
  Italiano, 31
  Quick, 29
  Rarebit-Style, 28
  -Sour Cream, 29
  Variations,
    Classic, 33
  Wines To Use in, 33
Chef's Salad in a
  Roll, 71
Cherries Jubilee, 64
Chi Chow,
  Oriental, 73
Chicken
  Aloha, 55
  Bacon-Wrapped, 9
  -Egg Foo Yong, 92
  Fantasia, 55
  Fondue, 16
  Salad, Herbed, 49
  Scramble, 76
  Wine-Broiled, 64
Chili-Cheese
  Sauce, 22
Chili con Cheese
  Dip, 46
Chinese Hot
  Mustard, 20
Chinese Hot Pot, 25
Chocolate
  Dot Waffles, 83
  Fondue, 34
  Haystacks, 71
  Mexican, 23
  -Nut Fondue, 34
Chowder au Vin,
  Clam, 50
Chuck Wagon
  Macaroni, 70
Cider Snap, 47
Clam Chowder au
  Vin, 50
Clam Dip, Creamy, 46
Classic
  Beef Stroganoff, 52

Classic *continued*
  Cheese Fondue, 26
  Cheese Fondue
    Variations, 33
Cocktail
  Hot Tomato, 47
  Meatballs, 8
  Sauce, 19
Cocoa, Breakfast, 85
Coconut
  Diamonds, 11
Corn Cakes,
  Double, 92
Corn Soup, Cream
  of, 47
Cottage
  Enchiladas, 55
Cottage Swiss
  Fondue, 28
Crab
  -Cheese Dip, 46
  -Cheese Fondue, 28
  -Potato Nibblers, 8
  -Stuffed
    Mushrooms, 48
Cranberry
  Sandwiches,
    Tuna-, 86
  -Sauced Bites, 44
  Sauce, Tangy, 20
Cream of Corn
  Soup, 47
Cream Squares,
  Fried, 36
Creamy
  Avocado Sauce, 22
  Catsup Sauce, 19
  Clam Dip, 46
  Ham Rolls, 57
  Ham Towers, 54
  Parmesan
    Fondue, 29
  Raspberry
    Fondue, 36
Crepes
  Grape-Syruped, 60
  Ham-Apricot, 54
  Suzette, 60
Crunchy Ham
  Sandwiches, 86
Crusty Vegetable
  Bites, 9
Curried Shrimp
  Skillet, 77

Curry
  Dip, Indian, 9
  Luncheon
    Shrimp, 76
  Sauce, 19
Custard French
  Toast, 92
Custard Soup,
  Japanese, 79

D-F

Daiquiri Blazer, 63
Delray Shrimp
  Dip, 44
Dessert Fondue
  Butterscotch, 36
  Caramel, 36
  Chocolate, 34
  Chocolate-Nut, 34
  Creamy
    Raspberry, 36
  Dippers, 34
  French-Toasted, 37
  Fried Cream
    Squares, 36
  Fruit Fritters, 37
  Ice Cream-and-
    Cake Cubes, 37
  Mini Pastries, 38
  Peppermint, 36
Deutsch Dinner, 55
Deviled Cheese
  Dip, 44
Deviled Steak, 74
Dill Sauce, 21
Dip
  Cheese and
    Bean, 10
  Cheese-Bacon, 44
  Chili con
    Cheese, 46
  Crab-Cheese, 46
  Creamy Clam, 46
  Delray Shrimp, 44
  Deviled Cheese, 44
  Duo Cheese, 46
  Elegante,
    Lobster, 44
  Hot Shrimp, 10
  Indian Curry, 9
  Sausage-
    Avocado, 10

Double Corn
  Cakes, 92
Dressing, Italian
  Parmesan, 90
Dumplings
  Blueberry, 62
  Quick Apple, 77
  Strawberry, 80
Dunk, Cheese and
  Bean, 10
Duo Cheese Dip, 46
Egg
  Foo Yong,
    Chicken-, 92
  Patties, Saucy, 89
  Eggwiches,
    Waffled, 82
Elegant Salmon
  Balls, 50
Enchiladas,
  Cottage, 55
Filled Lamb Balls, 18
Fish and Seafood
  Fondue, 15
Fish Fillets,
  Potato-, 76
Flank Steak,
  Fondued, 16
Fluffy Maple
  Sauce, 37
Fondue
  Beef, 15
  Beer Cheese, 29
  Buttermilk, 28
  Butterscotch, 36
  Caramel, 36
  Caraway-Cheese, 28
  Cheese-Sour
    Cream, 29
  Chicken, 16
  Chocolate, 34
  Chocolate-Nut, 34
  Classic Cheese, 26
  Cottage Swiss, 28
  Crab-Cheese, 28
  Creamy
    Parmesan, 29
  Creamy
    Raspberry, 36
  Dippers, Cheese, 26
  Dippers,
    Dessert, 34
  Fish and
    Seafood, 15

Fondue *continued*
  Flank Steak, 16
  French-Toasted, 37
  Ham, 16
  Italiano, 31
  Mexi-Meatball, 23
  Mini
    Pastries au, 38
  Peppermint, 36
  Pork, 16
  Quick, 29
  Rarebit-Style, 28
  Variations, Classic
    Cheese, 33
  Wines To Use in
    Cheese, 33
French
  -Fried Cheese, 12
  Mushroom
    Omelet, 70
  Toast, Custard, 92
  -Toasted Fondue, 37
Fried Cream
  Squares, 36
Fruit
  Fritters, 37
  Kabobs, Beef
    and, 68
  Medley, Hot, 62
Fruited Ham Balls, 8

G-L

Garlic Butter, 20
German
  Sandwiches, 87
Gingerettes, 83
Ginger Soy, 22
Glorified Rice, 90
Golden Raisin
  Flambe, 60
Grape-Syruped
  Crepes, 60
Green Goddess
  Sauce, 21
Green Salad
  Ensemble, 31
Green Salad
  Quintet, 57
Grilled Beef-
  wiches, 87
Grilled Salmon-
  wiches, 89

Ham
-Apricot Crepes, 54
Balls, Fruited, 8
Fondue, 16
in Sour Cream, 74
Rolls, Creamy, 57
Rolls, Stuffed, 74
Salad,
Cauliflower-, 75
Sandwiches,
Crunchy, 86
Towers, Creamy, 54
Hash-Browns, 80
Hash, Turkey, 77
Hawaiian
Pancakes, 89
Herbed Chicken
Salad, 49
Horseradish
Sauces, 20
Hot
Fruit Medley, 62
Pot, Chinese, 25
Shrimp Dip, 10
Tomato
Cocktail, 47
Ice Cream-and-Cake
Cubes, 37
Indian Curry Dip, 9
Italian Parmesan
Dressing, 90
Japanese Custard
Soup, 79
Japanese Tempura, 79
Jazzy Beef Bites, 18
Kabobs, Beef and
Fruit, 68
Kabobs, Lemony-
Shrimp, 68
Lamb Balls,
Filled, 18
Lobster
-Cheese Waffles, 82
Dip Elegante, 44
Newburg, 50
Luncheon Shrimp
Curry, 76

M-R

Macaroni, Chuck
Wagon, 70
Mandarin Pears, 61

Mapled Appetizers, 48
Maple Sauce, 37
Maple Syrup, 85
Marmalade Sauce, 21
Meat and Yam
Skillet, 76
Meatballs
Cocktail, 8
Crab-Potato
Nibblers, 8
Elegant Salmon, 50
Filled Lamb, 18
Fondue, Mexi- 23
Fruited Ham, 8
Jazzy Beef
Bites, 18
Reuben
Appetizers, 8
Spicy Appetizer, 38
Meat Fondue
Bacon-Wrapped
Chicken, 9
Beef, 15
Chicken, 16
Chinese Hot Pot, 25
Cocktail
Meatballs, 8
Crab-Potato
Nibblers, 8
Filled Lamb
Balls, 18
Fish and
Seafood, 15
Flank Steak, 16
Fruited Ham
Balls, 8
Ham, 16
Jazzy Beef
Bites, 18
Mexi-Meatball, 23
Pork, 16
Reuben
Appetizers, 8
Sausage
Meatballs, 16
Shrimp Toast, 9
Tiny Pronto Pups, 9
Veal Strips, 16
Menus
After-Ski
Scene, 31
Buffet Fondue, 10
Cooking on a Hot
Plate, 71

Menus *continued*
Dinner by
Candlelight, 57
Dinner on the
Move, 38
Dinner on the
Patio, 64
Dinner Oriental-
Style, 25
Fondue Fiesta, 22
Japanese
Specialty, 79
Just for the
Family, 80
Meal-on-a-
Griddle, 90
Self-Service
Supper, 49
Show-Stopping
Dinner, 58
Waffles for
Breakfast, 85
Wine-Tasting
Party, 12
Mexican Chocolate, 23
Mexican Hot
Sauce, 19
Mexi-Meatball
Fondue, 23
Mini Pastries au
Fondue, 38
Mocha Sauce, 63
Mushroom Omelet,
French, 70
Mushroom Sauces, 18
Mushrooms, Crab-
Stuffed, 48
Mustard, Chinese
Hot, 20
Mustard Sauces, 20
Newburg, Lobster, 50
Newburg, Shrimp, 50
Noodle-Bacon
Scramble, 54
Nut Fondue,
Chocolate-, 34
Nut Sauce,
Butterscotch-, 63
Nutmeg-Pineapple
Sauce, 63
Olive Sauce, 21
Omelet, French
Mushroom, 70
1-2-3 Sauce, 19

Onion
-Cheddar Soup, 47
Sauces, 21
-Wine Soup, 47
Oriental Chi Chow, 73
Original Caesar
Salad, 58
Oyster Stew,
Vegetable-, 71
Pancakes
a la Mode, 89
Double Corn, 92
Hawaiian, 89
Potato,   75
Parmesan Dressing,
Italian, 90
Parmesan Fondue,
Creamy, 29
Pastries au Fondue,
Mini, 38
Peach Betty, 63
Peach Sauce, 60
Peanut Sauce, 22
Pears, Cheese-
Filled, 62
Pears, Mandarin, 61
Peppermint
Fondue, 36
Pilaf, Tuna, 76
Pineapple
Delight Cake, 31
Sauce, Nutmeg-, 63
Sauce, Spicy, 21
Polka-Dot
Pinwheels, 12
Pork Fondue, 16
Potato
-Fish Fillets, 76
Hash-Browns, 80
Nibblers, Crab-, 8
Pancakes, 75
Pronto Pups, Tiny, 9
Quick Apple
Dumplings, 77
Quick Fondue, 29
Raisin Flambe,
Golden, 60
Rarebit-Style,
Fondue, 28
Rarebit, Western
Welsh, 53
Raspberry Fondue,
Creamy, 36
Red Sauce, 19

Relish, Sauce
a la, 21
Reuben Appetizers, 8
Rice, Glorified, 90

S

Salad
Cauliflower-
Ham, 75
Ensemble,
Green, 31
Herbed Chicken, 49
Original Caesar, 58
Quintet, Green, 57
Tangy Cauliflower
Bowl, 64
Salmon Balls,
Elegant, 50
Salmonwiches,
Grilled, 89
Sandwiches
Chef's Salad in a
Roll, 71
Crunchy Ham, 86
German, 87
Grilled Beef, 87
Grilled Salmon, 89
Polka Dot
Pinwheels, 12
Saucy Steak, 90
Sweet-Sour
Burgers, 80
Tuna-Berry, 86
Turkey Double
Decker, 86
Turkey Salad, 11
Waffled Egg, 82
Sauce
a la Relish, 21
Bearnaise, 19
Bordelaise, 19
Butterscotch-
Nut, 63
Caper, 21
Chili-Cheese, 22
Chinese Hot
Mustard, 20
Cocktail, 19
Creamy
Avocado, 22
Creamy Catsup, 19
Curry, 19

Sauce *continued*
Dill, 21
Ginger Soy, 22
Green Goddess, 21
Horseradish, 20
Marmalade, 21
Mexican Hot, 19
Mocha, 63
Mushroom, 18
Mustard, 20
Nutmeg-
Pineapple, 63
Olive, 21
1-2-3, 19
Onion, 21
Peach, 60
Peanut, 22
Red, 19
Spicy Pineapple, 21
Spicy Tomato, 19
Sweet-Sour, 19
Tangy
Cranberry, 20
Tartar, 21
Tomato, 19
Wine, 22
Saucy
Egg Patties, 89
Sausages, 48
Sausage-Avocado
Dip, 10
Sausage
Meatballs, 16
Seafood, *see also*
Meat Fondue
Fondue, Fish
and, 15
in Wine, 48
Shrimp
Cantonese, 70
Curry,
Luncheon, 76
Dip, Delray, 44
Dip, Hot, 10
Kabobs,
Lemony-, 68
Newburg, 50
Skillet,
Curried, 77
Sweet-Sour, 77
Toast, 9
Soup
Asparagus-
Cheese, 47

Soup *continued*
au Vin, Clam, 50
Cream of Corn, 47
Onion-Cheddar, 47
Onion-Wine, 47
Japanese
Custard, 79
Vegetable-
Oyster, 71
Sour Cream Fondue,
Cheese-, 29
Sour Cream, Ham
in, 74
Soy, Ginger, 22
Spicy
Appetizer
Meatballs, 38
Pineapple Sauce, 21
Tomato Sauce, 19
Steak
Deviled, 74
Diane, 58
Fondued Flank, 16
Sandwich,
Saucy, 90
Stew, Vegetable-
Oyster, 71
Strawberry
Dumplings, 80
Strawberry
Starter, 57
Stroganoff, Beer
Beef, 52
Stroganoff, Classic
Beef, 52
Stuffed Ham Rolls, 74
Sukiyaki, 74
Sweet-Sour
Burgers, 80
Sauce, 19
Shrimp, 77
Surprises, 49
Syrup, Maple, 85

T-V

Tangy Cauliflower
Bowl, 64
Tartar Sauce, 21
Tempura,
Japanese, 79
Tenderloin,
Burgundied, 53

Teriyaki
Appetizers, 68
Tiny Pronto Pups, 9
Toast
Cups, 55
Custard French, 92
Shrimp, 9
Tomato
Cocktail, Hot, 47
Sauce, Spicy, 19
Sauces, 19
Tuna
-Berry
Sandwiches, 86
Pilaf, 76
-Sauced Waffles, 82
Turkey
Double Decker, 86
Hash, 77
Saladwiches, 11
Veal
Bertrand, 53
Cordon Bleu, 69
Strips, 16
Vegetable Bites,
Crusty, 9
Vegetable-Oyster
Stew, 71

W-Z

Waffled Egg-
Wiches, 82
Waffles
Basic, 82
Chocolate Dot, 83
Gingerettes, 83
Lobster-Cheese, 82
Tuna-Sauced, 82
with Toppers, 85
Welsh Rarebit,
Western, 53
Wiener Schnitzel, 73
Wine
-Broiled
Chicken, 64
Guide, 32
Sauce, 22
Soup, Onion-, 47
Wines To Use in
Cheese Fondue, 33
Yam Skillet, Meat
and, 76